# THE RESTLESS EARTH

# LAYERS OF
# THE EARTH

# THE RESTLESS EARTH

Earthquakes and Volcanoes
Fossils
Layers of the Earth
Mountains and Valleys
Rivers, Lakes, and Oceans
Rocks and Minerals

# THE RESTLESS EARTH

# LAYERS OF THE EARTH

Krista West

THE FRANKLIN INSTITUTE

CHELSEA HOUSE
PUBLISHERS
An imprint of Infobase Publishing

# LAYERS OF THE EARTH

Chelsea House
An imprint of Infobase Publishing
132 West 31st Street
New York NY 10001

**Library of Congress Cataloging-in-Publication Data**
West, Krista.
  Layers of the earth / Krista West.
      p. cm. — (Restless earth)
  Includes bibliographical references and index.
  ISBN 978-0-7910-9706-9 (hardcover)
  1.  Earth—Juvenile literature. 2.  Earth—Crust—Juvenile literature. 3.  Earth—
Core—Juvenile literature.  I. Title.
  QE501.25.W47 2008
  551.1—dc22          2008027075

Chelsea House books are available at special discounts when purchased in bulk
quantities for businesses, associations, institutions, or sales promotions. Please
call our Special Sales Department in New York at (212) 967-8800 or
(800) 322-8755.

You can find Chelsea House on the World Wide Web at
http://www.chelseahouse.com

Text design by Erika K. Arroyo
Cover design by Ben Peterson

Printed in the United States of America

Bang EJB 10 9 8 7 6 5 4 3 2 1

This book is printed on acid-free paper.

All links and Web addresses were checked and verified to be correct at the time of
publication. Because of the dynamic nature of the Web, some addresses and links
may have changed since publication and may no longer be valid.

# Contents

▲ ▲ ▲

**1** The Dynamic Earth      7

**2** The Crust      18

**3** The Upper Mantle      29

**4** The Lower Mantle      44

**5** The Outer Core      59

**6** The Inner Core      69

**7** Studying the Earth      78

Glossary      88

Bibliography      93

Further Reading      97

Photo Credits      99

Index      100

About the Author      104

# The Dynamic Earth

▲ ▲ ▲

ON A QUIET WINTER MORNING IN JANUARY 2006, A GIANT, SLEEPING volcano on an unassuming, uninhabited island in Alaska awoke from a 20-year nap. And it woke up with a bang.

At about 4:44 A.M., the volcano known as Mount St. Augustine erupted, sending a cloud of steam and ash 45,000 feet (13,716 meters) into the air. Airplane pilots flying in the area quickly reported the eruption, and the Federal Aviation Administration temporarily restricted flights within 5 miles (8 kilometers) of the rumbling mountain. At the same time, the United States Geological Survey classified Augustine as an alert level red volcano, the highest level of concern. Everyone started to pay attention to Augustine.

The volcano continued to erupt for many days. Eventually, it sent a steam cloud to the southeast, over a 45-mile-long (75-kilometer-long) area. Amazingly, no one was hurt. To start with, no one lived on Augustine's remote island located in Alaska's Cook Inlet; the steam cloud never reached people living in the large, nearby city of Anchorage; nor did it clog the engines of unsuspecting airplanes passing by. Most people have never even

7

The subduction zone volcano Mount St. Augustine in Alaska woke up from its 20-year nap in 2006.

heard of the Augustine volcano. Augustine's eruption, however, is a sign that the dynamic Earth is still active.

The St. Augustine volcano, named by explorer Captain James Cook in 1778, is a classic **subduction zone** volcano. Subduction zones are usually located on the ocean floor; they are areas where one piece of Earth's surface slides below another piece into the interior of the planet. As the piece slides down, it absorbs the ocean water. Once this water-logged piece of land sinks below Earth's surface, the water comes into contact with the surrounding rock, causing it to melt. As a result, the deep, surrounding rock becomes much lighter than usual.

This pocket of light rock rises back towards Earth's surface like an ice cube floating up in a glass of water. On its journey to the surface, it melts the surrounding rocks and forms a bubble of

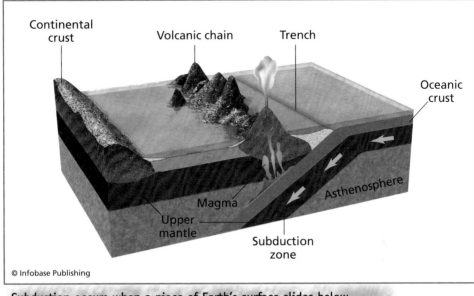

Continental crust
Volcanic chain
Trench
Oceanic crust
Asthenosphere
Magma
Upper mantle
Subduction zone

© Infobase Publishing

Subduction occurs when a piece of Earth's surface slides below another piece into Earth's interior. It is one of the many processes that help shape the planet's inner and outer layers.

liquid rock called **magma**. The magma supplies the lava that helps create a new volcano. With repeated eruptions of lava, steam, and ash at Earth's surface, a new subduction volcano is born.

Subduction is just one of Earth's many processes that have helped shape the planet's outer and inner layers over time. These processes have likely slowed since the planet first formed, but they have not stopped. Earth scientists work to understand how the surface of the planet changes shape. Their job is not always easy, and there is still much to learn.

## STUDYING EARTH'S LAYERS

All of Earth's layers have an impact on human life in some way. Some of the impacts are obvious, such as volcanic eruptions or life-threatening **earthquakes**. Others are not so obvious, such as the way in which the planet's magnetic field protects the Earth from the harmful energy in outer space. Obvious or not, human

# Earth's Layers

Depending where the lines are drawn, the Earth has five layers: the crust, upper mantle, lower mantle, outer core, and inner core. However, no one has ever actually seen the inner layers of the planet. Everything we know about Earth's interior has been deduced by scientists gathering information at the Earth's surface.

Thanks to this scientific research, humans now know the basic ingredients and general size of each of Earth's layers. Some of the layers are solid like an ice cube, while others are semi-liquid like a milkshake. Each layer is active and constantly changing.

Movements of rock and heat inside each layer give rise to different Earth processes. These processes help shape the planet as we know it, as indicated in the following table:

## Layers of the Earth

| | INGREDIENTS | APPROX. % OF PLANET | THICKNESS | MOVEMENT/ PROCESS |
|---|---|---|---|---|
| Crust | Basalt and granite | 0.5% | 3-43 miles (5-70 km) | Earthquakes |
| Upper mantle | Peridotite | 13% | 217 miles (350 km) | Plate tectonics |
| Lower mantle | Silica, some iron | 55% | 1,553 miles (2,500 km) | Convection |
| Outer core | Liquid iron | 30% | 1,367 miles (2,200 km) | Magnetic field |
| Inner core | Solid iron | 1.5% | 746 miles (1,200 km) | Heat generation |

life is directly affected by the processes that take place inside the Earth.

The study of Earth's layers ultimately helps humans to better understand the planet's processes, including those taking place in its inner layers. Generally known as **Earth science**, this field includes many different areas of scientific research. For example, a geologist studying rocks on a mountain is one kind of earth scientist; another type of earth scientist is the seismologist who records the waves of energy that travel through the Earth following an earthquake.

Despite the many forms of Earth science, however, there are really only two ways to study the Earth: with direct or indirect observations. Because the Earth cannot be easily recreated in a laboratory, scientists must look to the real world either directly (with their own eyes) or indirectly (through the eyes of scientific instruments).

## Direct Science

**Direct science** uses real, concrete examples that can be observed, measured, and studied with the human eye. Dissecting a frog to learn about its biology is a form of direct science. So is measuring the speed of a ball as it falls through space. In Earth science, geologists often use direct science to understand the history of the planet.

Geologists have determined the age of Earth's surface, for example, by using radioisotopes. A **radioisotope** is the radioactive form of an **element**; that is, the atoms of that element slowly lose particles—a process called decay—thereby turning into a different element entirely. Different types of radioactive elements decay at predictable rates.

By directly measuring how much of a certain element has decayed inside rocks on Earth's surface, scientists can determine the approximate age of that rock. Take two of the same rocks of different ages. The rock with only half of the amount of the original element remaining is twice as old as the rock with all of the element present. By measuring the decay of elements, scientists can determine the age of Earth's rocks.

This method of direct science is also called radioactive dating or radiometric dating, and is an important tool in the field of Earth science.

## Indirect Science

**Indirect science** uses tools and instruments to look and listen without observing something directly. One example of indirect science is a doctor's use of a stethoscope—an instrument—to listen to the heart. The heart is rarely ever seen directly.

Much of what scientists know about the inner layers of the Earth comes from indirect science. **Seismology**, for example, is the study of waves of energy traveling through the Earth, a field that plays a big role in the Earth sciences. Seismologists use tools such as seismographs, which measure these waves, to learn about different planet-shaping events. By studying the natural and human-made waves of energy that travel through the layers of the Earth, seismologists can learn much about the processes taking place inside the planet.

## WHEN IT ALL BEGAN

About 5 billion years ago, our Sun condensed out of a cloud of hydrogen gas and dust. Rotating around the newly formed star was a disk of material that was rich in elements. Over a period of about 500 million years, the material in the disk spread out and began to clump together to form the planets. Planets that formed from heavier elements clustered in closer to the Sun, while those that formed from lighter elements traveled farther out into space. During this time, the Earth formed as one of the four heavier, inner planets.

At first, the Earth was no more than a giant ball of hot, melted, mixed-up rock—unsorted and unorganized. This early Earth had no breathable air, no life, no oceans, and none of the familiar landscapes seen today. But as time passed, the Earth changed.

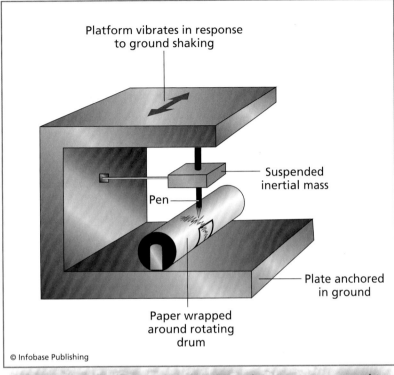

Platform vibrates in response
to ground shaking

Suspended
inertial mass

Pen

Plate anchored
in ground

Paper wrapped
around rotating
drum

© Infobase Publishing

Seismographs, the older cousin of modern seismometers, were used to measure waves of energy traveling through the Earth.

On the outside of the planet, the atmosphere formed and the oceans condensed. Inside the planet, the rocks began to cool and settle out into more organized layers. Some of the melted rocks began to solidify. Others naturally grouped together with rocks of their own kind. The most dense and heavy of these rocks sank to the center of the planet while the less dense, lighter, molten rock floated to the surface. Over hundreds of millions of years, the planet began to harden and take shape, while settling into three main layers: the core, the mantle, and the crust.

Earth's layers can be imagined as a hard-boiled egg. The familiar layers in a hard-boiled egg are the shell, the squishy white part, and the hard yellow yolk. The shell is thin, brittle, and cracks easily; the white part is thick, soft, and squishy; and the yolk is a solid and tightly packed ball. Earth's layers are not all that different.

# Is Earth Alone?

Evidence for the existence of other Earth-type planets in outer space may not come in the form of little green alien visitors but instead be found in the rocks known as **meteorites** that fall to the planet's surface. Meteorites are evidence of other rocky planets that may not have survived as the Earth did.

Most meteorites come in three forms: stony, iron-based, and stony-iron mixtures. Stony meteorites often resemble the rocks found on Earth. Iron-based meteorites are made mostly of slowly-cooled iron, as might be found in the core of a planet or large asteroid. The third type of meteorite, known as a "stony iron," has both Earth-like rocks and slow-cooled iron. These rare meteorites seem to have come from the boundary between a planet's iron core and its rocky outer layer.

The ingredients that make up these meteorites provide important clues that point toward the existence of planets with Earthlike layers, because these ingredients could not have formed in space on their own. The only way such meteorites could have been created, scientists suggest, is on an Earthlike planet. Evidence suggests that a small, rocky planet may have formed elsewhere and then broken up, dispersing pieces of Earthlike rock through space. When these rocks fall to Earth, they become meteorites.

Earth, it seems, was not the only rocky, layered planet to be created in our solar system. But it may be the only survivor.

## Core

If the Earth is like a giant, hard-boiled egg, then the core of the Earth is like the yolk. As the planet cooled, the heavy iron contained in the mix of melted rock started to separate out to collect as a core at the center of the planet.

According to some earth scientists, core formation happened very early in the history of the Earth, perhaps within the first hundred million years after the planet formed. During this period, a solid, inner core and a semi-liquid outer core took shape. Most scientists believe this inner core is still heated by warmth left over from the collision and accretion of the many asteroids and meteors (called **planetesimals**) that originally formed the planet.

Scientists now estimate that the Earth's solid-iron, inner core is about 746 miles (1,200 km) across, about the same size as the moon. The liquid-iron, outer core is about 1,367 miles (2,200 km) across. The inner and outer cores together make up about 30% of the Earth by volume.

## Mantle

Comparing the Earth with a giant, hard-boiled egg means the mantle is like the egg's thick, squishy white part. As the planet cooled and the heavy iron fell to the center, the lighter **silicate** rocks floated in the mantle above. Silicates include all kinds of rocks, usually containing the elements silicon and oxygen. Earth's mantle is believed to be made up of mostly silicate rocks.

Rocks in the mantle look more like those typically found at the Earth's surface. However, these rocks are kept warm by both the decay of radioactive elements and by the heat from the core. Because they are also subjected to pressure from the crust above, they tend to be semi-liquid, or viscous. The mantle, like the core, is thought to have formed very early in the history of the Earth.

Scientists now estimate that the thick-flowing mantle is about 1,800 miles (2,900 km) thick—taking up about 70% of the Earth by volume. Many earth scientists divide the mantle into the upper and lower mantle based on the properties and behaviors of the different rocks.

## Crust

If the Earth is a giant, hard-boiled egg, then the crust of the Earth is like the thin, brittle eggshell. Unlike the core and the mantle, the Earth's crust did not form from heavy and light elements that separated themselves early in Earth's history. Instead, the crust is constantly formed, destroyed, and reformed by processes happening inside the mantle.

The rocks in Earth's crust are primarily basalts and granites. **Basalts** are gray or black, fine-textured, heavy rocks. **Granites** are not-so-heavy pink, gray, or black rocks. The crust contains many other elements including sodium, aluminum, potassium, and iron.

Today, scientists estimate that Earth's crust is only 22 miles (35 km) deep on average. At its thickest points, the crust is no more than 50 miles (70 km) deep.

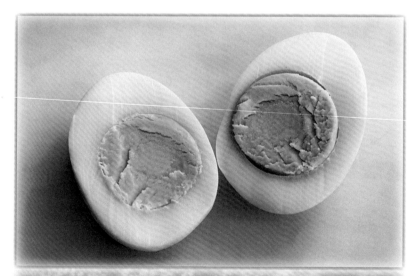

If comparing the Earth to an egg, the core would be the yolk (*above*). The Earth is made up of layers of varying thickness (*opposite*).

By first understanding how the Earth formed, then studying the processes that constantly shape the layers of the Earth, scientists are discovering more and more about the planet. And there is still much to discover. No one, for example, knows exactly when a volcano will erupt; how violently an earthquake will shake; or why the planet's magnetic poles move around. For Earth scientists, many mysteries remain to be solved.

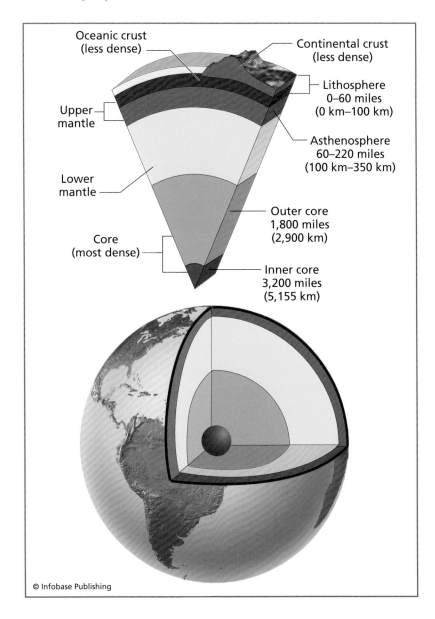

Oceanic crust (less dense)

Continental crust (less dense)

Lithosphere 0–60 miles (0 km–100 km)

Upper mantle

Asthenosphere 60–220 miles (100 km–350 km)

Lower mantle

Outer core 1,800 miles (2,900 km)

Core (most dense)

Inner core 3,200 miles (5,155 km)

© Infobase Publishing

# The Crust

▲ ▲ ▲

THE CRUST OF PLANET EARTH IS, AS DESCRIBED IN CHAPTER 1, LIKE THE shell of a hard-boiled egg: very thin and very hard compared to the inner layers. And, like an egg's shell, the crust is quite crackable.

When Earth's crust cracks, an earthquake happens. Over time, these earthquakes have helped to shape the planet's crust. They help build mountains, create oceans, and sculpt all the land in between. Earthquakes happen all the time, all over the Earth, and can be both visible and invisible to humans. But earthquakes are not random events. They happen for a reason.

Earthquakes are the end result of complicated forces and processes taking place inside the crust. On the surface, the crust may look fairly stable and still most of the time. A mountain, for example, does not usually move a lot. But inside the crust, big sections of rock are constantly moving and shifting. In fact, the whole crust is constantly changing and moving.

## CRUST BASICS

To understand how earthquake processes shape the crust, it helps to first understand a bit more about what makes up the crust.

## Thickness

The Earth's crust is a relatively thin layer of rock that is part of Earth's **lithosphere**. Its thickness varies a little depending on its location on the planet's surface. The crust under the oceans is thin, measuring between 3 and 6 miles (5 and 10 km) thick. The crust under the land, particularly under mountains, is much thicker, measuring between 12 and 50 miles (20 and 70 km) thick.

At its thickest point, a car moving at highway speed toward the center of the Earth would arrive at the bottom of the crust in about an hour. That's a quick drive.

Driving at the same speed through all of Earth's layers to the center of the planet would take more than 76 hours. That one-hour drive through the crust indicates that the crust is very thin compared to the area covered in the 76-hour drive to the planet's center.

## Ingredients

Earth has two types of crust: oceanic crust and continental crust. **Oceanic crust**, the layer found beneath the oceans, is made up of rocks called basalts. These gray or black, fine-textured, dense, heavy rocks are squeezed out of underwater volcanoes. Though these volcanoes are not easily seen, the ocean floors are full of them.

**Continental crust** is the layer of crust that makes up dry land and is made largely of rocks called granite. Granites are pink, gray, or black rocks that have melted and solidified on Earth's surface over time. Compared to basalts, granites are very light and loosely packed.

## Age

Oceanic crust is much younger than continental crust because oceanic crust is constantly being made and destroyed as under-water volcanoes erupt to make new oceanic basalts and add new rocks to the oceanic crust. During this process, certain areas in the ocean floor, called subduction zones, pull the older, heavy oceanic crust back into the interior of the Earth, destroying it.

The rate at which this ongoing process of creating and destroying oceanic crust occurs means that none of these rocks are very old—none of the oceanic basalts are more than 100 million years old. While this may sound like forever in terms of human history, most of the oceanic crust was formed during the last 2% of

# Weathering Reshapes New Hampshire

In May 2003, the state symbol of New Hampshire—a 40-foot-high (12 m) natural rock that resembled a human profile—toppled off the side of the mountain where it had stood for millions of years. The "Old Man of the Mountain" that graced the state's license plates, quarters, and souvenirs was no more.

The natural destruction of the "Old Man of the Mountain" is one example of the processes that shape the crust of the Earth. However, this event was not caused by a dramatic, jolting earthquake but by the slow, steady process of rock weathering.

**Weathering** is the breaking down of rocks on Earth's surface by wind, water, heat, and pressure. By this process, a large chunk of rock, like the rock face that turned into the "Old Man of the Mountain," is broken into smaller and smaller pieces of rock and helps shape the crust. In some cases, weathering results in soft, rounded river stones. In other cases, weathering results in dramatic changes in the shape of mountains.

New Hampshire's "Old Man of the Mountain" was formed naturally from five layers of granite rock. The structure toppled after the weathering process slowly wore down the bottom layers of granite

Earth's history. That means if the Earth were only 5 years old, the basalts would be only a few hours old.

The continental crust is much older than the oceanic crust. While it is constantly being created, it is rarely destroyed. Melted rocks from beneath the crust rise to the surface (either through volcanoes or other openings in Earth's crust) and solidify into granites, adding new rocks to the continental crust. But because these rocks are so light, they rarely sink deep enough into the

that supported the rock structure. For a long time, people were aware that weathering was weakening the Old Man, but no one was able to stop this natural process from taking its course.

Today, many visitors to the site leave flowers as a token of remembrance for the "Old Man of the Mountain."

(a)

(b)

The natural process of rock weathering slowly weakened New Hampshire's "Old Man of the Mountain." The picture on the left (a) shows the mountain before the rock face fell; the picture on the right (b) shows how it looked afterward.

oceans to reach the subduction zones where they would be destroyed.

As a result, continental crust rocks are a lot older. They can be as much as 3.8 billion years old (that's 38 times older than oceanic crust rocks). Again, if the Earth were only 5 years old, the granites would be only a couple of weeks old. That's a lot older than the oceanic crust, but still young when compared to the entire history of the planet.

## FORCES IN THE CRUST

All the rocks in Earth's crust—both oceanic and continental—are under constant **stress**, a force that causes the crust to change its shape, size, and location. The exact amount and type of stress varies. Stress at the surface of the Earth comes from the layers below the crust, deep in the upper mantle. Stress takes three basic forms: stretching, smashing, and shearing

### Stretching

**Tension** is the force that stretches the crust apart, making it thinner in the middle.  Over time, this action can create giant valleys and basins. The Great Basin, located between Utah and California, is one example of a low spot on Earth's surface that was created by tension forces.

### Smashing

**Compression** is the force that pushes the crust together, squeezing it until it folds or breaks. This folding action formed Earth's mountain ranges. The central Appalachian Mountains in Pennsylvania, for example, were created by compression forces that folded Earth's crust.

### Shearing

**Shearing** is the force that pushes a piece of rock in two opposite directions, causing a break or change of shape. Sheared areas of Earth's crust can form large areas of raised, flat land that are called plateaus. One example is the Colorado Plateau, a raised area of land that covers the corners of Arizona, Utah, Colorado, and New Mexico.

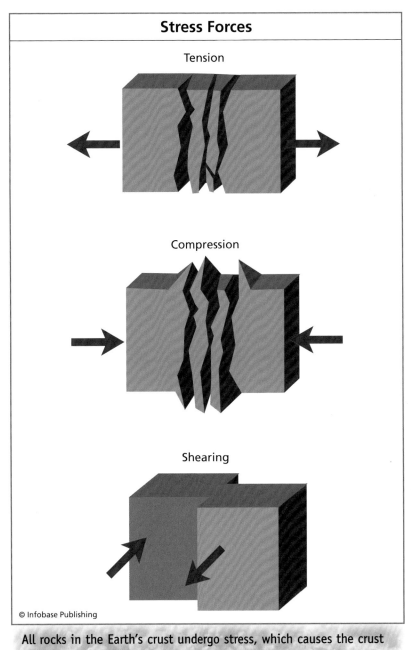

**Stress Forces**

Tension

Compression

Shearing

© Infobase Publishing

All rocks in the Earth's crust undergo stress, which causes the crust to change in different ways.

## EARTHQUAKES IN THE CRUST

With enough stretching, smashing, or shearing, the rocks in Earth's crust will simply break apart. Some solid rocks can stretch and stretch like a piece of taffy, but all rocks will eventually break. Once broken, the rocks in the crust are free to move much faster and cause earthquakes.

Scientists call a break in Earth's crust a **fault**. There are three basic forms of faults: normal faults, thrust faults, and strike/slip faults.

## Normal Fault

A **normal fault** happens when tension forces stretch the crust apart. When the fault stretches to its breaking point, the rocks suddenly move along the direction of the force and cause an earthquake. A normal fault breaks the crust at an angle so that one piece of rock slides up and one piece of rock slides down. The rocks that slide up can become mountains or plateaus; the rocks that slide down can become **rifts** or river valleys.

The Rio Grande Rift, stretching from Mexico through Texas and New Mexico, and into Colorado, is an example of a normal fault at a rift valley. The Rio Grande Rift is a low-lying river valley that is undergoing tension forces that are slowly pulling the rocks apart. The valley results from the downward-moving side of a large normal fault that is shaping the crust.

A **fault-block mountain** is a type of mountain created when two normal faults line up next to each other. This creates two breaks in the crust parallel to each other, forming a loose block of rock between the breaks. The loose block moves upward to form a mountain, while the surrounding rocks move downward.

One example of a fault-block mountain range is the Franklin Mountains, which run from north to south, splitting the west Texas city of El Paso down the middle. The fault-block range itself is thrust upward relative to the adjacent rock units immediately east and west of the range.

# Thrust fault

A **thrust fault** happens when compression forces smash the crust together. When the rock breaks, it breaks at an angle similar

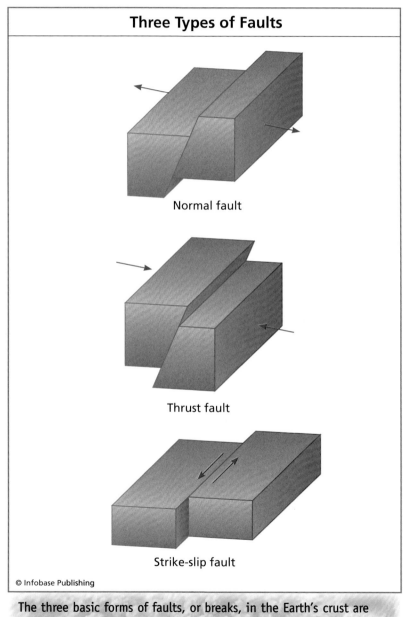

## Three Types of Faults

Normal fault

Thrust fault

Strike-slip fault

© Infobase Publishing

The three basic forms of faults, or breaks, in the Earth's crust are shown above.

to the normal fault. But in this case, the rocks move up and down in opposite directions of the normal fault movements. Thrust faults, sometimes called reverse faults, also create mountains and rifts on Earth's surface.

Many of the mountains in Southern California are the result of thrust fault movements. The San Gabriel Mountains, for example, are being pushed up and over the rocks of the San Fernando and San Gabriel valleys by a thrust fault. Parts of both the Rocky Mountains and the Appalachian Mountains are also formed by thrust faults.

## Strike/Slip Fault

A **strike/slip fault** happens when shearing forces slide rock units past each other horizontally, in opposite directions. In this

# Measuring Crustal Movement: Mark Zoback, Geophysicist

Researcher Mark Zoback is currently co-leading a project to dig a 1.9-mile-deep (3 km), vertical hole into the Earth. The goal of this project is to be able to directly measure earthquakes by actually placing instruments inside a fault, the place in the Earth where two pieces of crust break and move against each other.

Zoback is a geophysicist, a scientist who studies the physics of the Earth, at Stanford University in California. His project is part of EarthScope, a five-year project designed to learn more about the forces and processes that shape North America.

When the drill hole is completed, scientists will be able to directly measure earthquakes along California's famous San Andreas Fault, an 800-mile-long (1,300 km) break in the Earth's crust. On one side of this fault, one piece of Earth's crust is moving north. On the other side of the fault, another piece of the crust is case, there is little up and down motion. Instead, when the rock breaks, the two pieces of land slide past each other in a side-by-side motion. Unlike normal and thrust faults, strike/slip faults do not create obvious mountains and valleys. But they do cause some big earthquakes.

The San Andreas Fault, running roughly 800 miles (1,300 km) through much of California, is a famous example of a large strike/slip fault. Here, the westernmost crust of the California coastline is slowly slipping north as the eastern part of the crust slips south. Not surprisingly, this area is famous for its frequent earthquakes.

According to the United States Geological Survey Web site that describes the San Andreas Fault, these two pieces of California crust have moved past each other at least 350 miles

moving south. As these pieces slide past each other, earthquakes result.

These earthquakes, like all earthquakes, can only be measured and understood indirectly. Scientists can record and listen to waves of movement in the Earth during and after a quake, but they can never measure the movements in the fault directly. The new EarthScope hole, known as the San Andreas Fault Observatory at Depth (SAFOD), will change all that.

Zoback says SAFOD could revolutionize earthquake science, possibly helping people predict when and where an earthquake will occur. "Our current knowledge of fault-zone processes is so poor that not only are we unable to make reliable short-term earthquake predictions, we don't know whether such predictions are even possible," Zoback said in a Stanford University news report. "SAFOD could revolutionize our understanding of earthquake physics. By making continuous observations directly within the San Andreas Fault zone at depths where earthquakes start, we will be able to test and extend current theories about phenomena that might precede an impending earthquake."

(563 km) in the past 20 million years at a rate of about 2 inches (5 cm) per year.

## UNDERSTANDING THE EARTHQUAKE PROCESS

The basic causes of earthquakes in the planet's crust are well understood. This knowledge allows scientists to identify earthquake-prone areas and assess potential hazards. But the exact size and timing of an earthquake is virtually impossible to predict.

For example, scientists studying the crust in a given location can predict whether or not an earthquake is likely to occur in the next century. But they cannot tell you whether that earthquake will happen next week or next year. Earthquakes remain unpredictable for now.

Nevertheless, scientists know that the movements on the planet's surface often depend on the layer of Earth just below the crust, an area called the upper mantle. Earth's crust floats on top of the mantle almost like a boat on water. The processes that take place inside the upper mantle ultimately control when and how earthquakes happen.

# The Upper Mantle

▲ ▲ ▲

THE UPPER MANTLE OF PLANET EARTH LIES JUST BELOW THE CRUST. IT IS not considered a solid, but is thought of as being more like a very thick, slow-moving, and flexible liquid.

Riding on top of this liquid is the land where all life is found. The land, or crust, is created by molten rocks in the mantle that rise to the surface of the planet where they cool. While the upper mantle flows, it also moves the crust around the Earth's surface in a process known as **plate tectonics.**

Plate tectonics is a scientific *theory*, or a testable idea, that explains how the continents on Earth's surface move around. The plate tectonics process is responsible for the shape of the continents, the size of the oceans, and, ultimately, where earthquakes occur in the crust. Like many of Earth's processes, plate tectonics cannot be easily seen in action on a day-to-day basis, but it is a force that constantly shapes the planet.

## UPPER MANTLE BASICS

To understand the key role played by plate tectonics, it helps to learn a bit more about the composition of the upper mantle and the processes that take place within it.

## Thickness

The upper mantle is 217 miles (350 km) thick, contains two different types of rock, and is divided into two sections called the lithosphere and the **asthenosphere**. The rigid lithosphere is composed of a rocky crust that is 40 miles (64 km) thick and floats on top of the asthenosphere. The asthenosphere is 124 miles (200 km) thick, warm (2,640 °F or 1,449 °C), softer than the lithosphere, and is the more plastic section of the upper mantle. (The name comes from the Greek word *asthenes*, which means "weak.") Because of the temperatures and pressures that occur at this depth, the asthenosphere behaves like a very thick liquid.

## Ingredients

The lithosphere is made up mainly of familiar, crustal rocks known as **peridotites**. A peridotite contains the mineral olivine, a yellowy-green rock with lots of iron and magnesium. Because peridotites are heavier than most of the other rocks found in Earth's crust, they tend to sink to the bottom of the crust and into the upper mantle.

The asthenosphere of the upper mantle is different from the lower mantle. This is because the deeper in the Earth, the higher the pressure and temperature. The higher pressures and temperatures that exist in the lower mantle cause the rocks there to be less stable. That is, they tend to change forms easily. No one knows exactly what asthenosphere rocks look like, but they tend to contain mostly silicon and magnesium, along with smaller amounts of iron, aluminum, calcium, and sodium.

## Age

So far, no one has been able to dig deep enough into the upper mantle and determine the exact age of its rocks. But sometimes the upper mantle rocks rise to Earth's surface. Take diamonds, for example; they are more than just valuable jewels—they provide information about the age of the rocks in the upper mantle.

A diamond is a pure-carbon rock that is naturally formed in the extremely hot, high-pressure conditions found in the Earth's mantle. The gemstones can form at depths as shallow as 93 miles (150 km) below the continental crust, but usually come from farther down in the upper mantle.

In certain locations, diamonds (and other rocks) erupt onto the Earth's surface from deep in the upper mantle through specialized volcanic vents called **kimberlite pipes**. Most of these pipes are found on land that is older than 1.5 billion years.

But the diamonds that are mined from these pipes are much older than the land. Some of them can be as old as 3.3 billion years—more than two-thirds of the age of the Earth itself. Other gems range in age between 1 billion and 3 billion years old.

Although scientists cannot date the exact age of the upper mantle directly, diamonds and other evidence suggest that the upper mantle is nearly as old as the planet itself.

## Forces in the Mantle

The upper mantle of the Earth boils like a pot of melted chocolate. In both the upper and lower mantle, **convection** is the driving force at work. Convection is the movement of heat and matter within a liquid.

For example, as melted chocolate heats up in the bottom of a pot, it becomes less dense and lighter, and rises up to the surface. At the surface, it cools, becomes dense and heavy again, and sinks back to the bottom. The continued addition of heat produces a convection cycle or current, moving the chocolate in a circular motion round and round in the pot as it warms and cools.

The same process happens in the upper mantle, which is being constantly heated by the lower mantle and the molten core at the center of the Earth. As the upper mantle heats up, the rocks become less dense and rise toward the top. Just below the crust, the rocks cool and become dense again, slowly sinking back toward the lower portion of the upper mantle. Over time, a convection current is created that moves the rocks in a circular motion round and round in the upper mantle. The convection current continues as long as heat is added to the system.

Now imagine adding a solid piece of a chocolate bar to the surface of the pot of melted chocolate. Eventually, the chocolate bar will be pushed aside (or perhaps pulled down) by the convection currents in the pot. The same process happens at the surface of the Earth.

On top of the upper mantle sits Earth's crust. Just as a solid chocolate bar is pushed along and then pulled down into the boiling chocolate by the convection current in the pot, so too is the Earth's crust pushed along and then pulled down into the upper

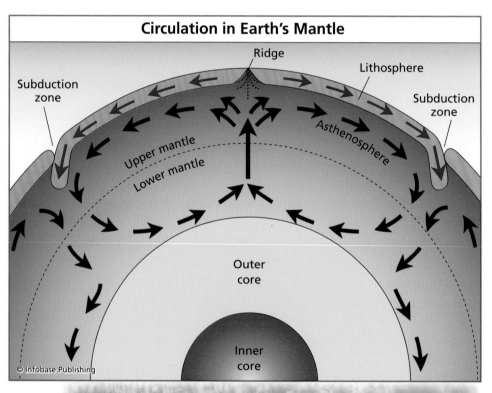

The convection current beneath the Earth's crust pushes the crust and pulls it into the upper mantle.

mantle by the cycle of the convection current that moves beneath the crust.

## PLATE TECTONICS

Plate tectonics explains the movements and the current location of Earth's continents. Ultimately, plate tectonics is explained by the convection currents in the upper mantle that move the crust around the planet to form the continents as we know them today.

Long before geoscientists understood plate tectonics, it was noted that Earth's land masses seemed to fit together like puzzle pieces. But no one had an explanation of the process to show how the pieces were connected in the past. However, in the time since reliable evidence for plate tectonics has developed, much more has been learned about the upper mantle's role in shaping the planet's surface.

## Tectonics History

In fact, going back as far as the 1700s, many people have noticed how the edges of Earth's continents seem to fit together. Benjamin Franklin, for example, was one of these observers, but he had no evidence to prove that the continents had once been connected, nor that they moved in chunks over the surface of the planet.

It was not until 1915 that the first real evidence for plate tectonics came to light. A German scientist named Alfred Wegener collected information on fossils, landforms, and climate to support an idea that he called **continental drift**. This idea proposes that Earth's continents were once joined together in a single mass before breaking apart to float around the surface of the planet. But while Wegener had some evidence that the continents moved, he had no explanation of how and why this happened; in other words, no mechanism to explain continental drift. As a result, the idea was never widely accepted by the scientific community.

Alfred Wegener died in 1930. But 30 years later, a mechanism for explaining continental movements came to light when scientists started to map magnetic variations in rocks lining the mid-ocean ridges located on the ocean floor. A **mid-ocean ridge** is an underwater mountain range where the Earth's crust moves apart while new oceanic rocks rise to Earth's surface from below. A **magnetic variation**, in this case, is the direction magnetic minerals in a rock are pointing.

A magnetic mineral always points north, but over time, Earth's north pole moves. In fact, the north and south poles have switched places repeatedly over time due to changes in Earth's magnetic field. A magnetic rock that is formed when the magnetic north pole is in its present position will point to what we now know as north. A magnetic rock formed when the north magnetic pole was in present-day south will point to what we now know as south.

In the 1960s, scientists developed the first map of the magnetic rocks—and the directions in which they pointed—that exist on the ocean floor. This map showed a zebralike pattern of symmetrical stripes on either side of the mid-ocean ridges. One stripe contains rocks whose magnetic minerals point to present-day north. The next stripe contains rocks with magnetic minerals that point to present-day south. This perfect pattern of stripes covers the entire ocean floor.

To explain their findings, scientists developed the idea known as **seafloor spreading**. As Earth's crust spreads apart at mid-ocean ridges, new rocks are formed by the intruding magma that rises from the upper mantle. As these newly emerged rocks cool, the magnetic minerals contained in them point toward whichever direction is north. Over time, the seafloor spreads apart. As magnetic north switches places on Earth, the direction of newly forming north-pointing rocks switches as well. Each stripe retains the magnetism it gained when it originally formed. Ultimately, this movement creates stripes of rocks with magnetic minerals that point in different directions.

Armed with the magnetic map and an explanation for seafloor spreading, scientists now had evidence to prove that continents moved along Earth's surface and a mechanism to show how. But if new rocks were constantly being added to the seafloor, somewhere on the planet the old rocks had to be destroyed (or else the planet would just blow up like a balloon). This lead to the discovery of

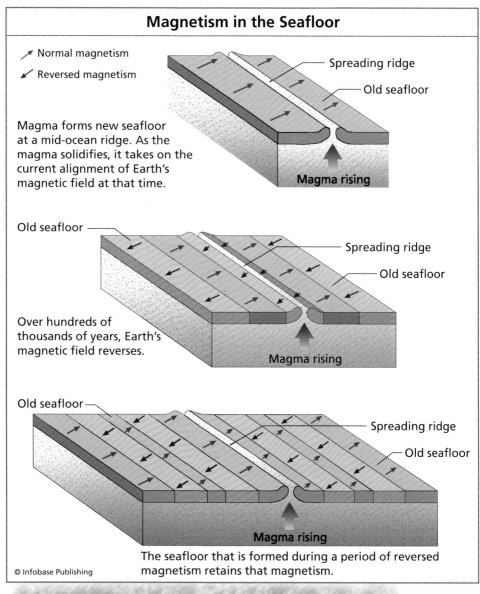

**Magnetism in the Seafloor**

↗ Normal magnetism

↙ Reversed magnetism

Spreading ridge

Old seafloor

Magma forms new seafloor at a mid-ocean ridge. As the magma solidifies, it takes on the current alignment of Earth's magnetic field at that time.

**Magma rising**

Old seafloor

Spreading ridge

Old seafloor

Over hundreds of thousands of years, Earth's magnetic field reverses.

**Magma rising**

Old seafloor

Spreading ridge

Old seafloor

**Magma rising**

The seafloor that is formed during a period of reversed magnetism retains that magnetism.

© Infobase Publishing

Magnetism in the seafloor indicates the reversal of Earth's magnetic field over time.

plate tectonics—arguably the most important process on the entire planet—a process that is driven by convection current movements in the Earth's upper mantle.

## The Plates

With the discovery that new rocks were constantly being created at mid-ocean ridges, scientists realized that Earth's crust is broken into moving pieces called **plates**. To picture Earth's plates, first picture a cracked, hard-boiled egg.

When someone drops a hard-boiled egg, its shell cracks into pieces, but the pieces are still held together by the squishy white

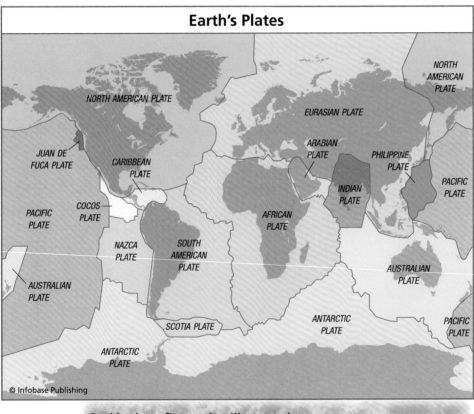

**Earth's Plates**

NORTH AMERICAN PLATE

EURASIAN PLATE

ARABIAN PLATE

PHILIPPINE PLATE

JUAN DE FUCA PLATE

CARIBBEAN PLATE

INDIAN PLATE

PACIFIC PLATE

COCOS PLATE

PACIFIC PLATE

AFRICAN PLATE

NAZCA PLATE

SOUTH AMERICAN PLATE

AUSTRALIAN PLATE

AUSTRALIAN PLATE

SCOTIA PLATE

ANTARCTIC PLATE

PACIFIC PLATE

ANTARCTIC PLATE

© Infobase Publishing

Earth's plates fit together like a puzzle.

of the egg. In the same way, the lithosphere of Earth's crust is cracked into plates that are separate but held together by the upper mantle. Each plate carries land, ocean floor, or both.

According to the United States Geological Survey Web site, the Earth has more than a dozen different plates. The exact number of plates depends on where scientists draw the plate boundaries, or edges. Most maps of the world include the African Plate, Arabian Plate, Antarctic Plate, Australian Plate, Caribbean Plate, Cocos Plate, Eurasian Plate, Indian Plate, Juan de Fuca Plate, Nazca Plate, North American Plate, Pacific Plate, Philippine Plate, Scotia Plate, and the South American Plate.

Some plates are huge, such as the Eurasian and North American Plates. Others are small, such as the tiny (but destructive) Juan de Fuca Plate. As these plates move, they undergo push and pull at their boundaries, often causing trouble for the people who live near them.

## Plate Movements

Unlike the broken pieces of a hard-boiled eggshell, Earth's plates are constantly moving around slowly on the surface of the planet. Most geologists believe that the convection currents in the upper mantle create the major forces that drive plate movements on Earth.

Earth's plates rest on the liquid rocks of the upper mantle. As these liquid rocks cool and sink, they pull the edges of the plates down into the mantle. The rest of the plate is dragged slowly along. The upper mantle's convection current continues to drag and move the plates on Earth's surface.

Different plates move at different speeds, but they all move very slowly by human standards—anywhere from 0.4 to 9.5 inches (1 to 24 centimeters) per year. The North American and Eurasian plates, for example, are moving apart at a rate of almost 1 inch (2.4 cm) per year, about the rate that human fingernails grow.

## Plate Boundaries

The edges of the plates on Earth's surface are called **plate boundaries**. Scientists group plate boundaries into three different categories based on how they are moving relative to each

# Plate Boundary Vacations

There are a few places on Earth where one can actually see the upper mantle pulling two pieces of Earth's crust apart. The island country of Iceland is one of them.

Earth's oceans are full of mid-ocean ridges, places where the plates are diverging and new crust is being formed. Most of these ridges are hidden at the bottom of the ocean under thousands of feet of seawater. But Iceland is one of the exceptions.

The Mid-Atlantic Ridge runs down the center of Iceland from north to south. Here, the Earth's diverging plates can be easily seen as giant, dramatic cracks in the landscape. Inside the cracks, melted rock bubbles to the surface to form new crust.

Iceland also sits on top of a **hot spot**. A hot spot is a place in Earth's crust that is positioned right above an upwelling of magma in the upper mantle. When a hot spot breaks through the crust, flowing magma creates large amounts of new crust. Because of the hot-spot activity—including many active volcanoes and hot-water vents that blast through the rock—the Mid-Atlantic Ridge pops above sea level at this place to create the island of Iceland.

But if Iceland is too cold for taking that geological vacation, Hawaii provides another option. It is also an island created by a hot spot bubbling in the Earth's upper mantle. One thing is for sure: Hawaii is warmer than Iceland.

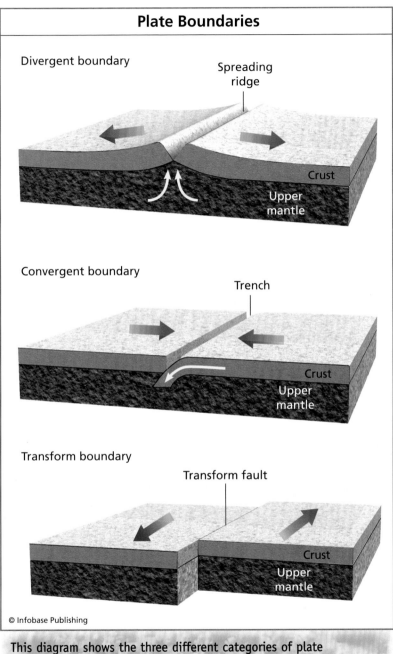

## Plate Boundaries

Divergent boundary

Spreading ridge

Crust

Upper mantle

Convergent boundary

Trench

Crust

Upper mantle

Transform boundary

Transform fault

Crust

Upper mantle

© Infobase Publishing

This diagram shows the three different categories of plate boundaries based on how they move in relation to one another.

other: convergent boundaries, divergent boundaries, and transform boundaries.

A **convergent boundary** is where two plates are moving towards each other, or converging. Depending on the density of the plates involved, one plate may slide below the other, or they may just smash together.

A plate slides below another plate because it is denser and heavier. If a plate carrying continental crust collides with a plate carrying oceanic crust, for example, the denser oceanic crust plate sinks beneath the lighter continental crust plate. This sinking plate slides down into the upper mantle. Rising temperatures in the mantle melt the sinking plate and destroy it. The area where this submergence and melting takes place is called a subduction zone.

In cases where plates of the same density collide—for example two continental plates—they will simply smash together to form a pile of wrinkled crust called a mountain range. One famous example of this collision is the smashing of the continental Indian Plate into the continental Eurasian Plate to form the Himalayan Mountains in Asia, home to some of the biggest mountains in the world—including 29,060-foot (8,850 m) Mount Everest.

A **divergent boundary** is where two plates are moving away from each other, or diverging, with new crust rising up to fill the gap. Many divergent boundaries are found along mid-ocean ridges where seafloor spreading takes place. As the ocean floor spreads open, new crust is formed as molten magma fills the open split. As the spreading and filling continue, wrinkling in the new crust often creates a ridge of underwater mountains.

When divergent boundaries occur on land, they often create deep valleys known as rift valleys. As two continental plates diverge, new crust is created to fill in the gap. The Great Rift Valley in eastern Africa, for example, is the result of the African Plate and Arabian Plate moving apart and new crust being formed. The Great Rift Valley varies in depth from nearly 1,000 feet (305 meters) deep to nearly 10,000 feet (3,000 m) deep in Kenya.

The famous San Andreas Fault is a transform boundary where the Pacific Plate slides past the North American Plate.

A **transform boundary** consists of two plates that slip and slide past each other in opposite directions. With this type of boundary, the crust is neither destroyed nor created. Instead, it just gets pushed around a lot in fairly unpredictable ways. As a result, earthquakes are quite common along transform boundaries.

The San Andreas Fault in California, for example, is a transform boundary where the Pacific Plate slides past the North

# Understanding Tectonic Plates: Julie Elliott, GPS Graduate Student

A graduate student at the University of Alaska-Fairbanks, Julie Elliott studies the movements of tectonic plates in south central and southeast Alaska. Here, several tectonic plates are smashing into each other to create dramatic mountain ranges and multiple volcanoes. The mystery is that no one knows exactly where or how these plates start and stop.

To help understand the movements of the Earth in this region, Elliott takes **Global Positioning System (GPS)** measurements at about 70 sites. These instruments record very accurate measurements of any location on Earth's surface. By taking multiple measurements over many years, Elliott can see the directions of the plate movements and try to explain those movements by using mathematical models.

Elliott, who is pursuing a doctorate degree (Ph.D.), started out by first completing her bachelor's degree in physics in college. She became hooked on plate tectonics when she took a geology class during her third year of school and decided to apply her physics expertise to this area.

Today, most of Elliott's GPS sites in Alaska are accessible only by helicopter, plane, or boat. She spends summers visiting the sites and taking new measurements. Besides getting to her sites, "the biggest challenge to doing fieldwork is getting the wildlife to leave the equipment alone. The bears of Alaska chew up cables and solar panels, disconnect batteries, and knock over the mounts the GPS antennas sit on," she says. "They seem to think I've personally delivered new toys to them."

American Plate. The San Andreas Fault is one of the most famous and closely observed land features on the planet, largely because of its impact on the population of California.

In 1906, an earthquake along the San Andreas Fault struck the city of San Francisco hard, killing nearly 3,500 people and destroying hundreds of buildings. Since then, the area has prepared itself better for earthquakes while the population has steadily grown.

## UNDERSTANDING THE PLATE TECTONICS PROCESS

It has taken scientists centuries of work to figure out the basic process of plate tectonics. Like many things in Earth science, the causes and effects of plate movements are known, but the exact details are a mystery. The more the details of the upper mantle are understood, the more scientists can help develop tools to make it safer to live in tectonically active, earthquake-prone places on Earth.

To really understand plate tectonics, scientists must probe even deeper into Earth's layers, down past the upper mantle. The lower mantle, the next level down, is more than 1,500 miles (2,500 km) thick. Convection forces in this layer of the planet affect the two layers above it, ultimately helping to shape Earth's surface in sometimes destructive ways.

# The Lower Mantle

▲ ▲ ▲

JUST BELOW THE UPPER MANTLE OF THE EARTH'S INTERIOR LIES THE
lower mantle. This area is also like the squishy white of a hard-
boiled egg. The lower mantle is more solid than the upper mantle,
but it still moves very slowly like a very thick liquid. Two main
processes that shape the planet take place in the lower mantle—
one of them is visible to humans, while one is not.

First, the lower mantle plays a major role in forming and
fueling volcanoes. Hot convection forces in this layer slowly boil
liquid rocks and minerals until they explode through Earth's crust
as volcanoes. That is the visible part.

Second, the lower-most part of the lower mantle—the part
that bumps up against the outer core—may be a graveyard for
old continents. Here, scientists have detected a mysterious layer
hundreds of miles across that some suspect is made up of slabs of
continent-like rock—but no one knows for sure. This is the invisible part: No human eye can see into this "graveyard" or anything
else in the lower mantle. Instead, scientists "see" processes in the
lower mantle by using seismology, the study of waves of energy
and how they travel through the Earth.

## LOWER MANTLE BASICS

While the lower mantle is a mystery, seismology has helped provide some of the clues scientists need to solve it.

## Thickness

The lower mantle is the thickest continuous layer inside the Earth, ultimately making up more than 50% of the planet by sheer size, and more than 70% of the planet by mass (or weight). The lower mantle measures about 1,550 miles (2,500 km) thick and has temperatures as high as 4,000 °F (2,204 °C).

## Ingredients

Scientists believe that the lower mantle is made mostly of magnesium, silicon, and oxygen, with smaller amounts of iron, calcium, and aluminum.

Together, the magnesium, silicon, and oxygen form a lower mantle mineral known as perovskite, probably one of the most common mineral ingredients inside the Earth. This mineral can also be found in Earth's crust, but it is extremely rare.

## Age

The exact age of lower mantle rocks is difficult to determine because the rocks cannot be reached for sampling. But because we know this layer formed very early in the history of the Earth, it means the rocks are probably billions of years old.

At the same time, lower mantle rocks change their forms slowly and regularly as the layer convects and boils. Older rocks can be changed into new, younger rocks through convection. All rocks at this depth are highly susceptible to convection.

## FORCES IN THE LOWER MANTLE

As it is in the upper mantle, convection is the main force that drives the movement of heat and rocks in the lower mantle. In fact, scientists suspect that the lower mantle contains one giant layer of convecting rocks.

Remember that convection is the movement of heat in a liquid, like a boiling pot of melted chocolate. Because hot melted

# The Integrated Ocean Drilling Program

Imagine sticking a straw into a thick wedge of watermelon, putting a finger over the end of the straw, and pulling out a thin sliver of watermelon. This thin sliver is a *core* of the watermelon, which provides a sample of the fruit at different depths. In a similar manner, scientists take cores from the ocean floor to learn about processes in the lower mantle, but they use a much, much bigger straw—a deep-ocean drill.

The Integrated Ocean Drilling Program (IODP) is an international program that sends ships out to sea that, quite simply, drill holes into the seafloor and extract a core of the Earth's crust that they label and store for later study.

Each of these cores contains all sorts of information that is useful to scientists; they basically provide a history of conditions on Earth's surface. The deeper parts of the core contain dirt and sediment deposited in the past. The shallower parts of the core contain more recent Earth samples. Cores may hold clues to Earth's past climate and old volcanic eruptions, and may even provide a detailed fossil record of ocean life.

Scientists gather clues to what's happening inside the lower mantle by extracting and studying core samples in areas near underwater volcanoes. Because processes in the lower mantle feed the volcanoes on Earth's crust, core samples from these areas contain rocks and minerals from the lower mantle. By studying these volcanic cores, scientists can learn about what's happening inside the invisible lower mantle.

chocolate (or rock) is less dense and light, it rises to the top of the pot. Cooler melted chocolate (or rock) is more dense and heavier, so it sinks to the bottom of the pot where it gets slowly heated. As long as heat is added to the system inside the Earth, the hot rock will rise and the cool rock will sink, creating a circle of roiling, melted rocks.

On the upper edges of the lower mantle, closest to the surface of the Earth, these convection forces form and fuel many of the world's volcanoes. On the lower edges of the lower mantle, closest to the core of the Earth, convection appears to drag chunks of continent down where they are stored like sunken spoons sitting at the bottom of a pot of melted chocolate.

## VOLCANOES

Volcanoes are vents over weak spots in Earth's crust where hot, liquid rock rises to the surface. Sometimes the liquid rock explodes out of the volcanoes in a dramatic eruption. At other times, the volcanoes sputter out ash and steam. Essentially, volcanoes exist to release heat and rock from the lower mantle. As a result, the volcanoes on Earth's surface provide one way for scientists to learn about the lower mantle.

Not all volcanoes work the same way. Scientists classify different types of volcanoes depending on how they are formed and fueled. Earth scientists currently believe that most volcanoes form when unusually hot rocks in the lower mantle push through the upper mantle toward the planet's surface.

### Shield Volcano

A shield volcano neither looks nor acts like a typical volcano. They look more like a big bump beneath Earth's surface, with gradual, sloping sides that can stretch for miles and miles. They erupt slowly and steadily over time, rather than with a big, sudden boom.

Shield volcanoes are fueled mainly with melted basalt that oozes slowly and steadily from a spot in the lower mantle. Eruptions can take place on and off, slowly, for many, many years.

Lava, or melted rock, seeps out and cools to gradually create giant, gently sloping mountains.

Mauna Loa in Hawaii is the Earth's largest shield volcano. According to the Hawaii Center for Volcanology Web site, Mauna Loa has erupted nearly 40 times since the early 1800s and measures 60 miles (97 km) long and 30 miles (48 km) wide. Like other shield volcanoes, it poses few immediate dangers to humans because the sluggish, steady nature of its lava flow gives those who live in the area plenty of warning time to evacuate.

Shield volcanoes are also common on other planets. Venus, for example, has more than 150 large shield volcanoes that look much like shield volcanoes on Earth. Mars is home to Olympus Mons, the largest shield volcano in the solar system—an enormous structure larger than the state of Colorado.

## Cinder Cone

A cinder cone is a pile of ash and rock pieces that often contains trapped bubbles of volcanic gas. Cinder cones usually look soft and round, with large craters at the center. The sides of cinder cones are too weak for big, inner bubbles of lava to spout out the top, so instead the lava often flows out the sides.

Cinder cones are usually found near volcanic vents, areas on Earth's surface where the mantle releases heat and gas. Cinder cones pop up most often on the sides of larger shield volcanoes, where the lower mantle seems to need another place to vent its heat. But cinder cones can also arise in unexpected places.

The most famous example of an unexpected cinder cone is a small mountain in Mexico called Paricutin. Paricutin unexpectedly popped out of a Mexican corn field in 1943 from a new volcanic vent. Eruptions continued for nine years, built the cinder cone to a height of 1,391 feet (424 m), and produced lava flows that covered 16 miles (25 km).

## Stratovolcano

A stratovolcano looks like the classic, pointy-peaked volcano that a child would draw. It is made of layers of ash, hardened lava, and other rocks that have built up over time.

Stratovolcanoes are also called composite volcanoes because they are fueled by two ingredients from the mantle: explosive eruptions of lava and quiet eruptions of ash and steam. As the volcano alternates between the lava and ash eruptions, it slowly builds up a mountain of layered materials. Because they erupt in different ways, stratovolcanoes can create unpleasant surprises for humans.

Mount St. Helens in Washington State is a classic example of a stratovolcano. In 1980, Mount St. Helens literally blew its top and destroyed nearly 230 square miles (595 square km) of forest and sent a cloud of ash thousands of feet into the air, according to the Mount St. Helens National Volcanic Monument Web site. The major 1980 eruption lasted for 9 hours. Since then, the volcano has been quietly spewing ash and steam, steadily and slowly building back its mountaintop. In 2004, lava erupted from the volcano, leading to a recent period of lava buildup. The alternating periods of lava eruptions and ash eruptions are what make the stratovolcano grow.

## Hot Spot Volcano

A hot spot volcano can occur on land or in the ocean, and often dramatically spews lava. It forms when bubbles of melted mantle rock break through Earth's crust.

Hot spot volcanoes are also known as mantle plumes. Scientists suspect the pipelike plumes stay in one spot inside the planet, sort of like a stationary straw, while the plates move along the surface above it. As the plates move over the mantle plumes, the melted mantle rock rises to create chains of volcanoes.

Yellowstone National Park in Wyoming, for example, is a hot spot under the North American Plate. As the plate slowly moves west and southwest, the stationary hot spot in the lower mantle pops a line of volcanic holes through Earth's crust. The last major eruption at Yellowstone occurred some 600,000 years ago. Yellowstone is one of only a few dozen known hot spots in the world. Another one is the Hawaiian Island chain, a series of shield volcanoes formed over a known hot spot that originates in the lower mantle.

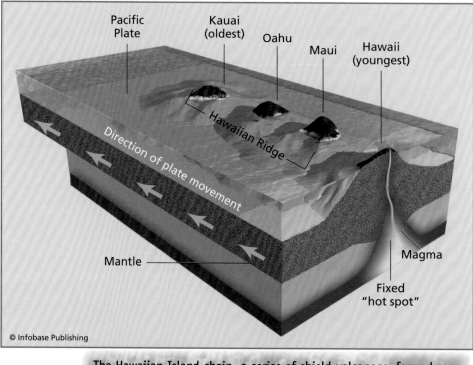

Pacific
Plate

Kauai
(oldest)

Oahu

Maui

Hawaii
(youngest)

Hawaiian Ridge

Direction of plate movement

Mantle

Magma

Fixed
"hot spot"

© Infobase Publishing

The Hawaiian Island chain, a series of shield volcanoes, formed over a hot spot that originates in the lower mantle.

## UNDERSTANDING VOLCANOES

Although scientists know a lot about volcanoes, they certainly have much more to learn. How to predict exactly when a volcano will erupt, for example, is not entirely understood. When an eruption does take place, scientists cannot yet predict how big it might be and exactly who will be affected on the land or in the sky. These two big questions are largely unanswered. If the lower mantle makes volcanoes tick, then understanding more about the lower mantle could help scientists understand more about the volcanic processes seen at Earth's surface.

No scientific tool currently exists to directly study the lower mantle because it is so deep inside the Earth. However, scientists commonly use seismology and Global Positioning System (GPS) instruments to draw conclusions about Earth's inner layers, including the lower mantle. By applying these tools at volcanic sites like Mount St. Augustine in Alaska, scientists hope to some-day predict the timing and size of eruptions.

## Seismology on Augustine

Seismology is the study of waves of energy traveling through the Earth. Instruments called seismometers record these waves of energy, and seismologists study the recorded waves created by volcanoes, earthquakes, and human-made explosions. The patterns and behavior of waves as they travel through the lower mantle can tell scientists about that layer. Certain waves, for example, travel only through solid rock and cannot pass through liquid rock. Scientists use this sort of information to draw conclusions about the composition of the invisible lower mantle.

When Augustine erupted in 2006, seismologists with the Alaska Volcano Observatory (AVO) at the University of Alaska-Fairbanks already had 15 seismometers in place to record the rumblings of the volcano and the surrounding rock. Using the information gathered by the seismometers, scientists have been watching Augustine volcano for many years.

Augustine erupted in 1986 and then went quiet for nearly 20 years. In 2005, AVO seismologists recorded a slow increase in earthquakes at Augustine—a clear sign that the volcano was preparing to erupt again. According to AVO data, Augustine experienced one or two earthquakes a day in early May 2005. By October, there were three to four earthquakes a day. And by mid-December, there were as many as 15 earthquakes in one day.

When Augustine finally erupted in January 2006, the AVO scientists were not surprised. They were waiting for Augustine to erupt. But they did not know how big the eruption might be and who would be in danger. Luckily, the 2006 eruption did not take any human lives. But next time could be different.

Seismologists are currently studying the 2006 eruption to learn more about the inner workings of Augustine.

## GPS on Augustine

GPS uses a network of satellites in space to communicate with GPS instruments on Earth to determine precise locations on the planet's surface. These instruments are often permanently anchored to the sides of a volcano, for example, where they can communicate their exact location to the space satellites. Whenever the land moves, the instruments move with it. Satellites in space record these tiny movements. GPS instruments do not directly study the lower mantle. But by recording movements at Earth's surface, scientists hope to understand more about the lower mantle forces that drive these movements.

# Listening to Earth's Movements: Maya Tolstoy, Marine Seismologist

Marine seismologist Maya Tolstoy is exploring new ways to listen to underwater volcanic eruptions and earthquakes. She focuses mainly on mid-ocean ridges, places in the deep sea where oceanic plates are moving apart and new crust is being created. At these places, volcanic activity and earthquakes are common—but they are often hard to see and hear.

Tolstoy is a marine seismologist, a scientist who studies energy waves as they travel through and beneath the Earth's oceans, at the Lamont Doherty Earth Observatory of Columbia University in New York City. Recently, Tolstoy began a study of specific energy waves in the oceans known as sound waves.

When a volcano erupts at a mid-ocean ridge, it is almost always accompanied by earthquakes. Together, the eruption and earthquake create the expected seismic waves—called **P waves** and **S waves**—that scientists often examine to learn about the layers of

Scientists currently operate five GPS instruments on the Augustine volcano to monitor the movements of the volcano's surface. Based on the information recorded by these GPS instruments so far, AVO scientists suspect that Augustine's magma chamber is growing. The sides of the volcano are slowly expanding, suggesting that the magma chamber is refueling—building up a new supply of lava—for another eruption.

In the past, Augustine has erupted in phases. One large eruption nearly empties its magma chamber, and that eruption is then followed by many, much smaller eruptions that help rebuild and refuel the mountain. At the moment, scientists are watching the volcano daily to see what it does next.

the Earth. But they also create a sound wave of energy found only in the oceans; this wave is called a T wave, or *tertiary wave*.

Tolstoy records these T waves using giant, underwater microphones known as hydrophones. T waves can travel thousands of miles underwater, so hydrophones often capture the sounds of all the earthquakes that happen in the world's oceans. At the same time, the hydrophones record all the other sounds in the ocean—including ship engines and whale songs—making a big jumble of recorded sound.

One of Tolstoy's biggest challenges is separating the T waves made from volcanoes and earthquakes out of all the other sounds recorded by the hydrophones. Once she has the seismic information she wants, it can help her and other scientists understand what happens at a mid-ocean ridge.

In the future, Tolstoy hopes to listen to the seismic waves in the ocean in real time (rather than recording them on a hydrophone and listening to the events after they happen). Tolstoy says: "We will be able to see things on the seafloor as they are actually happening. It's going to make such a difference to our understanding. And it already has in the areas where we have our real-time seismic monitoring."

One scientist, AVO's Jeff Freymueller, says that "capturing daily, even hourly, movements of volcanoes in real time brings a new dimension to volcano research." The hope is that such

# EarthScope: Understanding Layers of the Living Earth

The GPS instruments on the Augustine volcano are only a small part of a much larger science project called EarthScope. The main goal of EarthScope, according to its Web site, is to "explore the structure and evolution of the North American continent and understand processes controlling earthquakes and volcanoes." The federally funded, multimillion dollar project is the largest effort ever to understand the layers of the active Earth.

To meet its main goal, EarthScope scientists are using different tools to look at the Earth in North America. Each tool has a different research purpose. EarthScope is divided into three main projects that use these different tools: SAFOD, PBO, and the USArray.

SAFOD stands for the San Andreas Fault Observatory at Depth. This project's goal is to drill a 1.9-mile (3 km) deep hole into the planet's crust through California's 800-mile-long (1,300 km) earthquake zone. With such a hole in the crust, scientists could directly measure changes in the surface of the Earth during an earthquake for the first time in history.

PBO stands for the Plate Boundary Observatory. This project is designed to measure millimeter-scale movements of land near volcanoes and in earthquake zones using GPS instruments. When completed, PBO will include more than 900 instruments throughout the western United States and Alaska. Together, these instruments will measure how the land in these regions is shifting and stretching. PBO measures movements in Earth's crust to learn about processes in Earth's mantle.

in-depth monitoring will help scientists better understand the active Earth. Augustine is just one of the places that scientists are studying to learn more about volcanoes.

USArray (United States Array) is a grid of seismometers being set up like a moveable blanket over the United States. The seismometers will record waves of energy traveling deep inside the Earth's layers, including through the lower mantle. By the summer of 2007, USArray scientists had installed nearly 400 seismometers (out of about 1,000 total planned) in a grid over the western part of the country. Over the next 15 years, many of these instruments will "roll" over the country, moving from place to place and stamping out a grid of information taken all across the continent. USArray focuses on learning about processes in the upper and lower mantle.

Pictured here is the San Andreas Fault Observatory at Depth, or SAFOD—one of the tools used by EarthScope.

## THE CRUSTAL GRAVEYARD

Beneath the upper portion of the lower mantle lies what is known as the crustal graveyard—a mysterious layer in the lower-most part of the lower mantle. The crustal graveyard appears to be made of huge slabs of rock hundreds of miles across. Scientists call the layer the D" (short for "D double prime") layer.

The 120-mile-thick (193 km) D" layer was first detected and named by seismologists in the late 1940s. Ever since that time, scientists have been trying to figure out exactly what the layer is made of and why it is there.

One idea is that D" is made of old continental crust that was subducted by the mantle but never melted, eventually sinking and

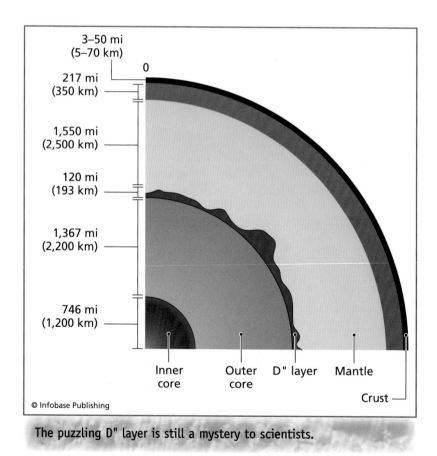

3–50 mi
(5–70 km)

0

217 mi
(350 km)

1,550 mi
(2,500 km)

120 mi
(193 km)

1,367 mi
(2,200 km)

746 mi
(1,200 km)

Inner core

Outer core

D" layer

Mantle

Crust

© Infobase Publishing

The puzzling D" layer is still a mystery to scientists.

becoming trapped at the bottom of the lower mantle. D" could be made of material that has welled up from the Earth's central core. It could be some new rock formed inside the Earth. Or it could be a graveyard of oceanic crust.

No one really knows the answer, but there is undoubtedly some process going on inside the lower mantle that forms and maintains the D" layer. Perhaps someday scientists will solve the mystery.

## P WAVES AND S WAVES

Virtually everything known about the crustal graveyard and the lower mantle comes from the science of seismology. "Seismos" is a Greek word meaning "shock." Seismology is literally the study of the Earth's "shocks."

Only a few things can cause the Earth to shake: large meteorites hitting the planet; human-made explosions; earthquakes; and volcanoes. Each of these occurrences is like throwing a pebble into a pond: They send waves of energy that travel out from the source in a predictable way.

By studying these waves of energy and how they travel inside the Earth, scientists learn more about what rocks are present and whether or not they are liquid or solid. There are two main forms of energy waves that travel through the Earth: P waves and S waves.

When an actual Earth-shaking event occurs, the first, fastest waves of energy that travel through the planet are the primary waves, or P waves. P waves compress and stretch the Earth from side to side like an accordion in the direction they are traveling. P waves move through solids and liquids. Sound waves that travel through the air are examples of P waves.

The second, slower waves of energy that travel through the planet after a shaking event are the secondary waves, or S waves. S waves move in two directions: from side to side and up and down. S waves are also known as shear waves. Waves in the ocean act like S waves.

While P waves can travel through both solids and liquids, S waves cannot move through liquids. When S waves hit a liquid inside the planet, they cannot be detected by seismometers. Scientists use the P and S waves of seismology to study interesting places in Earth's layers. The D" layer, magma pockets beneath volcanoes, and Earth's core were all discovered (and are now being studied) using seismology.

Seismologists have also been studying the area at the center of the Earth, beneath the lower mantle. This is an area that is part solid, part liquid, and rotates like a ball bearing inside the larger Earth. It is called the Earth's core.

# The Outer Core

▲ ▲ ▲

THE OUTER CORE OF PLANET EARTH LIES JUST BELOW THE LOWER MANTLE and is like the thick ring of greenish color that sometimes surrounds the yolk of a hard-boiled egg. But unlike the materials in the mantle that make it to the surface of the Earth daily, the materials in the outer core are not going anywhere anytime soon. Nevertheless, as far down in the earth as they are, the materials and the processes taking place inside the outer core still have an immense impact on human life. In fact, the outer core protects life on Earth.

## OUTER CORE BASICS

The outer core is made of melted, or molten, metal that is constantly in motion. This motion helps create the planet's **magnetic field**—the invisible force field that makes a compass point north and helps birds fly south. Perhaps more importantly than providing a means of navigation, the magnetic field protects the Earth from harmful things in space.

The Sun, for starters, can be harmful. It emits much more than just warmth and light; our planet's star is constantly sending out a broad flow of particles of energy called the solar wind. Most of the solar wind's particles carry electrical charges that can be harmful to humans and human-made things.

The planet's magnetic field, generated by Earth's core, protects the planet's surface from the solar wind. When the solar wind hits the magnetic field surrounding the planet, it gets deflected like water flowing around the bow of a ship. The potentially harmful energy particles flow past the Earth. Without the magnetic field, the Earth would be a much less inviting place to live.

## Thickness

The outer core is about 1,367 miles (2,200 km) thick. It is a bit thinner than the lower mantle, but it is still one of the thickest layers in the planet. Most of the Earth is made up of the lower mantle and outer core.

## Ingredients

With temperatures ranging from 4,000 °F to 9,000 °F (2,204 °C to 4,982 °C), the outer core, unlike other layers of the Earth, is molten metal. It contains mostly iron—the main ingredient in the steel used to make cars and ships—with a little bit of nickel. About 10% of it is made of other elements, most likely oxygen and sulfur.

No one has actually sampled the materials in the Earth's core. Its ingredients are assumed from two things: what seismology reveals about the size and density of the core, and what meteorites tell us about planet formation.

Iron is a heavy, dense metal that slows seismic waves traveling though the planet. Most of the solid planets in our solar system are believed to have solid cores made of iron and nickel, which are the main ingredients in iron meteorites. (Iron and nickel are the last elements created by large stars before they explode.)

## Age

The outer core is likely as old as the planet Earth itself, perhaps some 4.5 billion years old. Although no one knows for certain, some scientists suggest that the core formed within the first 100 million years of Earth's history.

## FORCES IN THE OUTER CORE

There are two main influences at work on molten metals in the outer core: **heat** and **gravity**. When heat and gravity interact with Earth's natural rotation in space, the metals in the outer core are able to flow and move in all directions.

Heat is a form of energy created by tiny movements of particles inside the elements. An object becomes hot when lots of particles within it move with lots of energy. An object is cold when there is little movement and little energy. The heat inside the Earth's outer core keeps the metals liquid, allowing them to move.

Gravity is the force of attraction between two objects that have mass. Gravity is what makes water flow downhill and a ball fall to the ground. In the Earth's outer core, gravity also makes the metals move.

Together, heat and gravity are influenced by the natural rotation of the planet. The Earth is constantly rotating, or spinning, like a slow-moving top. The time it takes for the planet to complete one full spin is what humans call a day.

Earth's daily rotation affects everything on the planet in some way—for example, it makes night and day and has an effect on wind and tides—but some effects are not so easily seen or explained, among them the impact of Earth's rotation on forces in the outer core. But the impact is real.

## THE MAGNETIC FIELD

The Earth itself is a giant magnet. Most people are familiar with small magnets—the pieces of metal that often decoratively cling to the refrigerator door. But not many people are aware that the Earth is a giant magnet with its own magnetic field.

The planet's magnetic field is not completely understood, but is thought to be a layer of moving, electrical charges surrounding

# The Fingerprint of the Magnetic Field

Humans have the Earth's magnetic field to thank for the aurora borealis and aurora australis, which are also known as the northern and southern lights. The auroras are moving displays of light in the night sky. They can be red, green, blue, or a mix of colors, and are most commonly seen near the north and south poles of the planet.

Auroras occur when solar wind particles hit Earth's magnetic field and are redirected toward the planet's poles. At the poles, these solar

Colorful auroras, like the one seen here, occur when collisions of gases and solar wind particles take place in Earth's atmosphere.

the Earth. Magnetic fields cause the tiny particles inside elements to line up in predictable and patterned ways. All magnets have a magnetic field, but some fields are much stronger than others. Magnetic fields allow refrigerator magnets to stick, make

wind particles interact with gases in Earth's atmosphere and release energy as light particles, which are called **photons**.

Depending on what type of gas is involved and how high in the atmosphere the collision occurs, different colors of light are produced. Red auroras occur when collisions take place at very high altitudes; green lights occur in the middle; and blue lights occur when collisions take place at lower altitudes. According to some calculations, at least 100 million collisions must occur between solar wind particles and atmospheric gases for an aurora to be visible from Earth's surface.

But just as Earth is not the only planet that has a magnetic field, it is not the only planet that has aurora displays. As long as a planet has a magnetic field and an atmosphere, it will have auroras not that different from those on Earth.

Jupiter and Saturn, for example, have their own aurora displays. Also, like Earth, these auroras tend to form in ovals surrounding the poles of the planets. The oval auroras can be seen in photographs taken in space as small circles of light, like large halos encircling each pole. In many cases, these auroras are not the red, green, and blue colors typical to Earth. Instead, they are often made of ultraviolet light that can be seen only in special photographs.

To see an earthly aurora, it is best to travel to the northern or southern end of the planet when the nights are dark and the Sun has been most active, emitting lots of solar wind particles caused by solar storms and solar flares. The more particles, the more chances there are of seeing a large and dramatic aurora display.

compasses point north, and protect planets from harmful streams of energy in space. The Earth's magnetic field exists because of the processes happening inside the outer core. Without the magnetic field of Earth, the planet would not be what it is today.

## The Geodynamo

The Earth's outer core actually is a **geodynamo**, a mechanism that creates the magnetic field of a planet. Today on Earth, the geodynamo makes north point north and south point south.

It takes three forces to make the Earth's geodynamo work: motion, electricity, and a magnetic field. Whenever motion and electricity are present, a magnetic field will be created. The outer core of the planet has all three.

The liquid iron in the outer core is constantly in motion. The force of the planet's heat and gravity, combined with the natural rotation of the planet, keep the melted metal moving.

The liquid iron on the outer core also has electricity. Technically, electricity is nothing more than moving charged particles. The particles that make up the iron in the outer core are naturally charged—that is, they have a positive or negative charge—and they are moving.

As a result, the outer core generates a magnetic field and, because the outer core is so large, the magnetic field is also very large: It is big enough to extend far beyond the planet and out into space. Ultimately, Earth's magnetic field does two things: It provides a way for humans to tell direction, and it protects the planet from harmful things in space.

## Pointing Direction

When a magnetic field is in action, the particles in that field will always point in a certain direction, usually called north. Sometimes the direction of the magnetic field is obvious and useful, sometimes it is not.

A compass is a tool that makes the Earth's magnetic field obvious and useful for navigation because of how its needle always points towards the planet's north pole. Humans have used compasses (and the outer core's magnetic field) to navigate since at least the twelfth century.

Less obvious, but still quite useful, at least to geologists, is the direction in which the metallic materials contained in rocks are pointing. When new rock rises to the surface of the Earth as magma, all the metals contained in that rock line up pointing north, and they stay pointing north as long as the rock is solid. This information can help scientists understand when a rock reached Earth's surface.

## Protecting the Planet

The electrical currents that make up Earth's magnetic field act as a shield that protects the planet from the Sun's solar wind, the steady stream of particles that bombard everything in space. When the solar winds reach the Earth, the magnetic shield

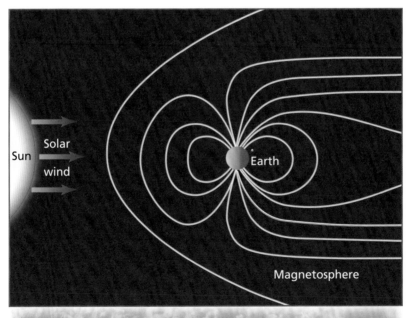

The Earth's magnetic field protects our planet from the Sun's solar wind, which could have damaging effects if it hit the Earth directly.

deflects the potentially harmful particles toward the planet's poles. Most of the solar wind particles never reach the surface of the planet.

Without the protective shield created by the outer core's magnetic field, life on Earth would be different. A stream of solar wind hitting the Earth could do a lot of different things: It could impact human electrical systems on Earth's surface, scramble satellite-based communications in space, and temporarily widen the hole in the protective layer surrounding the Earth, known as the ozone hole.

## Switching Poles

On average, Earth's north and south poles switch places every 250,000 years. During these times, the magnetic field of the Earth reverses itself over many thousands of years so that north becomes south and south becomes north.

Earth's last pole reversal was about 780,000 years ago. But this does not mean humans should expect a sudden switch anytime soon. At times in the past, the Earth has gone for 35 million years without switching its poles. No one knows exactly why switches happen—but it is all related to processes in the outer core.

One idea that might explain magnetic field reversals focuses on the boundary between the lower mantle and the outer core. Here, some scientists suggest, pockets of iron become trapped. If the magnetism of these trapped iron pockets is oriented in the opposite direction from the magnetism of the Earth, it may spread and influence the rest of the core. Eventually, this could cause a magnetic field reversal. But no one knows for sure.

Many scientists are studying and measuring the Earth's magnetic field to learn more. The strength of the field was first measured in the 1830s, using magnetic observations combined with mathematical equations, by Carl Friedrich Gauss. Gauss first defined the unit of magnetism that measures magnetic field strength (the gauss), then developed a mathematical method to measure the magnetism of Earth's field. Today, the magnetic field is about 10% weaker than when Gauss first measured its strength. But because it will likely take thousands of years to reverse, scientists are not worried.

# Modeling the Earth: Gary Glatzmaier, Computer Modeler

Computer modeler Gary Glatzmaier develops global, three-dimensional computer models to study planets and stars. A computer model is a large computer program where scientists can input known information and predict what might happen in the future for a given situation. Computer models are used to simulate events in the body, in the sky, and in the Earth.

Glatzmaier is a professor of Earth and planetary sciences at the University of California-Santa Cruz (UCSC) and was the first person to make a computer model that successfully simulated Earth's geodynamo.

By using Glatzmaier's geodynamo model, scientists learned a lot of new things about the Earth. The model showed one way that the magnetic field of the Earth might be generated by the outer core. It also showed how the magnetic field might flip its poles and reverse. The model also predicted that the Earth's inner core might rotate faster than the rest of the planet. This prediction was later confirmed by seismic observations and data.

Glatzmaier's current research focuses on the giant planets, including Saturn, and on the Sun. Models of the inside of the Sun have shown how waves of gravity in the Sun's interior may be affected by the outer edges of the Sun. In other work, Glatzmaier is creating computer models of volcanic eruptions on Earth's surface and in the mantle.

Glatzmaier hopes that each model will help scientists understand a little more about the layers of the Earth and how they work.

## UNDERSTANDING THE MAGNETIC FIELD

The usefulness of Earth's magnetic field—and the possibility of pole reversals—reminds humans that something as distant and invisible as the outer core can still impact life on the planet's surface.

Because the outer core of the Earth is not easily seen or measured, scientists use indirect methods to study its processes. Computer models, elaborate computer programs that simulate processes in the Earth, are commonly used to predict and understand core behavior. Seismology, the backbone of indirect Earth science, is used to study both the outer and inner core.

# The Inner Core

▲ ▲ ▲

THE INNER CORE OF PLANET EARTH LIES BELOW THE OUTER CORE, AND is like the solid yolk of a hard-boiled egg. Here, at the center of the Earth, temperatures reach up to 9,000 °F (5,000 °C), almost as hot as the surface of the sun. Scientists suspect much of this heat is left over from the planet's creation, and has been stored in the inner core for billions of years.

Although humans are largely insulated from the intense heat of the inner core, it still plays a big role in shaping the planet on a daily basis. The inner core's heat fuels the convection forces in the mantle, helping to make the surface-shaping processes like volcanoes and plate tectonics possible. Without the heat of the inner core, some suggest, Earth would have frozen solid eons ago.

## INNER CORE BASICS

Recently, there is evidence that the inner core is more than just Earth's heater. It appears the inner core is rotating on its own inside the planet, like a small planet inside a larger one. Scientists suggest that the inner core rotation probably has some effect on the planet's magnetic field, but no one yet knows its exact impact or importance.

## Thickness

The inner core is a solid ball about 746 miles (1,200 km) across, about the same size as Earth's moon. Unlike the other layers of the Earth, the inner core is a solid ball of metal. There are no other layers inside. The inner core is truly the center of the planet.

## Ingredients

The inner core has the same basic ingredients as the outer core: It contains mostly iron with a little bit of nickel, with the remaining 10% made up of other elements.

The inner core is not molten, but solid. This is because it is under huge amounts of pressure—about 930 pounds per cubic foot (15 grams per cubic centimeter), to be exact. That's about 14 million times the pressure felt by humans at Earth's surface. Under this amount of pressure, the molecules in the core do not have the freedom to move as a liquid would.

## Age

Earth's inner core, like the outer core, is as old as the planet itself. Some earth scientists suggest that the core formed within the first 100 million years of Earth's history. By this estimate, the inner core is about 4.5 billion years old.

## FORCES IN THE INNER CORE

The forces at work inside the inner core are largely a mystery. Because the inner core is a solid ball of metal, it is much different from the other layers of the Earth. There are no moving continents, convecting rocks, or hot spot volcanoes (or at least none have been found so far). The inner core is a decidedly different environment from the rest of the Earth's layers.

Scientists suspect there are two forces at work here: heat and electricity. While the heat left over from the planet's creation helps heat the Earth today, it comes as a slow seepage out from the inner core to the surface. Additionally, an electric current, generated largely by the movement of metals in the outer core, may be the force that drives the inner core rotation. But neither force is well understood. Yet, that is.

## THE INNER CORE'S HEAT ENGINE

All the layers of the Earth beneath the crust give off heat, including the inner core. According to Chris Marone, professor of geosciences at Pennsylvania State University, the layers beneath the crust produce enough heat to brew about 200 cups of hot coffee every hour for each of the planet's 6.2 billion people. This heat is not there by accident.

Some scientists believe that Earth's heat comes from four sources. The first two originate from the mantle: radioactivity and gravitational heat. After those two sources, there is leftover heat from Earth's creation, and heat from the expanding core. Although most of the planet's heat is in the mantle, the inner core is also an important source.

### Radioactivity in the Mantle

About 90% of the heat coming from inside the Earth, called **geothermal** heat, is caused by radioactive elements in the mantle. Elements are made up of atoms; each atom has a center called a nucleus.

The nucleus of one type of atom, called a radioactive atom, gives off pieces of energy until the nucleus reaches a stable point. At this stable point, the atom's energy is balanced and it stops moving. Elements in the mantle—including certain types of potassium, uranium, and thorium—are radioactive. As they give off energy, they heat the mantle and the rest of the planet. Radioactivity is responsible for generating much of the planet's heat.

## Gravitational Heat

**Gravitational heat** inside the mantle provides about 5% to 10% of the Earth's heat. It is created by the scraping and sliding together of rocks inside the Earth, sort of like when metal scrapes on a road to create sparks.

# When the Earth Becomes the Moon

Earth's moon is a cold, dead satellite. It likely formed billions of years ago when a chunk of debris the size of the planet Mars hit the Earth and knocked off a huge piece of rock. That rock eventually settled into orbit as the Earth's only moon.

As a result of its likely earthly origins, the moon contains many of the same rocks as Earth and even the same basic, layered inner structure consisting of a crust, mantle, and core. But the moon is missing other things that help make life on Earth possible, including an atmosphere, water, breathable oxygen, and—though it is not as noticeable to those of us living on top of the crust—core heat.

The moon does not have enough inner heat to maintain a living environment like the Earth. Temperatures on the surface of the moon fall to -243 °F (-153 °C) at night. The core of the moon is suspected to be cold as well, but no one knows the exact temperature.

As the Earth slowly loses its core heat to the mantle and the solid core grows, some say the planet is destined for a cold future. Some earth scientists speculate that, billions of years in the future, Earth's core will have cooled and grown enough to take over the mantle and meet the Earth's crust. By this time, they say, the Earth will be as cold and dead as the moon.

The force behind this scraping is gravity (which is why it is called gravitational heat). Gravity pulls dense, heavy rocks toward Earth's core. These rocks scrape and slide past other rocks on their way down. This scraping, or friction, contributes a small portion of the planet's heat.

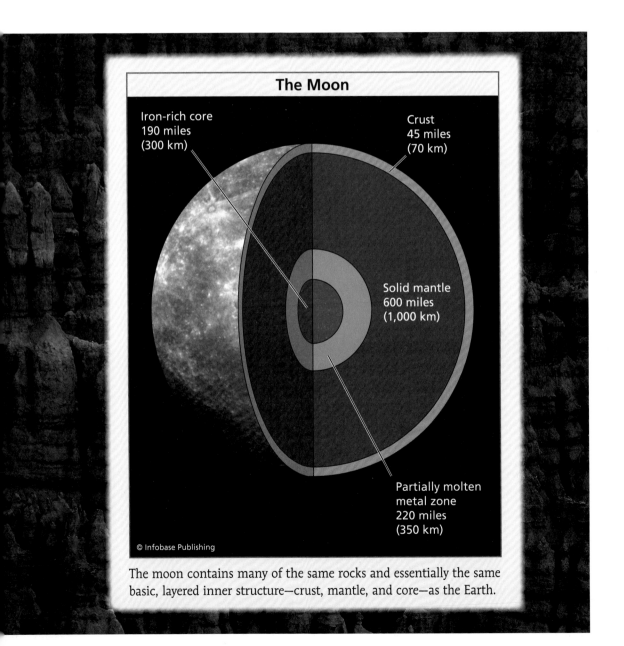

### The Moon

Iron-rich core
190 miles
(300 km)

Crust
45 miles
(70 km)

Solid mantle
600 miles
(1,000 km)

Partially molten
metal zone
220 miles
(350 km)

© Infobase Publishing

The moon contains many of the same rocks and essentially the same basic, layered inner structure—crust, mantle, and core—as the Earth.

## Heat Left Over from Earth's Creation

About 5% to 10% of the Earth's heat is left over from Earth's creation. This is sometimes called the Earth's "original heat." When the planet formed some 4.5 billion years ago, it was a boiling ball of gas and rock that has been cooling ever since.

The outer layer of Earth's crust cooled and hardened first (as does water in an ice-cube tray when the tray is filled and the water begins to freeze; the outer layers of each ice cube freeze and harden first). The crust trapped the rest of the original heat inside the planet. Because the core formed first, it holds much of the Earth's original heat.

## Core Expansion

The rest of Earth's heat comes from expansion of the inner core. The inner core grows by about .5 inches (1 cm) every 1,000 years. This growth is caused by the cooling of the outer core, which releases heat, and adds solid layers to Earth's center.

Just as liquid water turns to solid ice when it cools past a certain point, the liquid metal in the outer core also turns to a solid as it cools. This newly cooled solid is deposited on the outside of the inner core, slowly expanding the size of the inner core. The inner core grows by about 0.01 inches (0.3 mm) per year. In time, the inner and outer cores could fuse into a solid, cold ball of metal.

## THE INNER CORE'S ELECTRICITY

The Earth's inner core rotates on its own, faster than the rest of the planet, but no one really knows why. It was in the 1990s that scientists discovered that the inner core rotates faster than the rest of the planet. The Earth spins completely around—360°—in one day, while the inner core rotates a bit faster—about 3 extra degrees in one year. That means in about 120 years, the inner core completes one more lap than the planet Earth. What is the evidence for the idea that the inner core is rotating faster than the rest of the planet? The answer, like just about everything known about the inner core, comes, once again, from the science of seismology.

The iron in the inner core has a crystal-like structure. A **crystal** is an organized solid with its parts packed in specific patterns. Seismic waves in the Earth travel through the crystals of the inner core faster in one direction (north to south) than in the other direction (west to east).

By measuring the speed of seismic waves that travel through the inner core over many decades, scientists realized that the inner core is moving separately from the rest of the planet. This movment could be caused by the outer core's magnetic field seeping into the inner core and generating an electric current. If so, the current could drive the inner core's rotation.

But no one really knows what makes the inner core rotate on its own, and why it spins faster than the rest of the planet. There could be an electrical force at work, or there could be other factors.

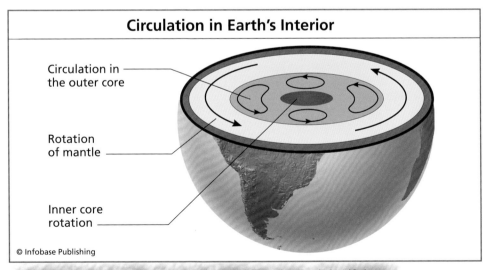

## Circulation in Earth's Interior

Circulation in the outer core

Rotation of mantle

Inner core rotation

© Infobase Publishing

The inner core of the Earth rotates faster than the Earth itself, but nobody knows why.

# Studying the Planets: David J. Stevenson, Planetary Scientist

Planetary scientist David J. Stevenson studies the origin, evolution, and structure of planets. He often uses the information collected by robots and probes in outer space to draw conclusions about what other planets are like and how they formed. But he occasionally thinks up crazy ideas about the inner Earth as well—including how to send a probe to the inner core.

Stevenson is a professor of planetary science at the California Institute of Technology in Pasadena, also known as Caltech. In 2003, Stevenson published a paper—largely, he says, just to get people thinking—about sending a probe to the Earth's inner core.

In the paper, Stevenson suggests that a probe could be "imbedded in a large volume of liquid iron alloy that migrates to the core along a crack propagating under the action of gravity." In other words, stick a probe in a bubble of liquid iron, and let the iron bubble carry the probe through cracks in the Earth to the inner core. According to this idea, the probe would take about a week to reach Earth's core, where it could send information back to the planet's surface using seismic waves.

Critics, of course, found many potential problems with the idea of sending a probe to the inner core of the Earth. The probe could freeze, overheat, be smashed to bits by pressure, fail to find the right "crack" through which to travel, or simply become lost in Earth's interior.

It may sound like a totally crazy idea, but as Stevenson says, the "same could be said about space mission designs years before the missions flew."

Philip N. Froelich, the director of the School of Earth and Atmospheric Sciences at the Georgia Institute of Technology, once told *Scientific American*, "I suspect that if you ask 100 geophysicists this question [why the inner core rotates faster than the rest of the Earth] you will get 99 different answers, and at least one of them will turn out to be right!"

# Studying the Earth

▲ ▲ ▲

STUDYING AND UNDERSTANDING THE OUTER AND INNER LAYERS OF planet Earth is not an easy task. The comparison with the hard-boiled egg ends here.

Studying the details and processes inside a hard-boiled egg is easy. An egg can be handled, observed, measured, manipulated, and tested in all sorts of ways. It can be compared to other hard-boiled eggs. It can be torn apart and dissected without fear of destroying anything that cannot be easily replaced by boiling another egg. There is an almost endless supply of hard-boiled eggs available to science.

But the study of the details and processes inside the Earth is truly difficult. While some parts of the planet can be handled, observed, measured, manipulated, and tested directly, most of the rest is completely out of reach and out of sight. As a result, scientists often have to take a creative approach to Earth science.

Generally speaking, an Earth scientist is someone who studies the Earth. But there are many different disciplines within Earth science, each focused on different layers of the Earth.

This naming convention may not seem familiar, but it is not unusual. A medical doctor, for example, may do many different things. One doctor could specialize in open-heart surgery while another doctor treats teenage acne; other doctors care only for injured animals. Each of these doctors has a very different education and purpose. But they are all called doctors.

The same kind of categories apply to Earth science. An Earth scientist can specialize in studying the rocks in the crust, measuring the iron content of seawater on the planet's surface, or measuring the energy deep in Earth's core. Each of these Earth scientists has a very different education and purpose. But they are all known as Earth scientists

Someone interested in becoming an Earth scientist should first get a feel for the many scientific disciplines in the field. Different disciplines look at different layers of the Earth. Many focus on the Earth's crust, simply because that is the easiest layer to study. And most of the disciplines have *geo* (meaning "Earth") in the first syllable of their name.

## GEOLOGY

**Geology** is the study of the solid matter in the Earth, including the history of and processes that shape the rocks, soils, oils, and gemstones contained in Earth's crust. Most geologists spend much of their time studying actual rocks in a laboratory.

To study a rock, geologists often first make a thin, almost transparent section of the rock they wish to study. Next, they glue it to a glass slide and view it under a microscope while shining different types of light through it.

Different types of rock appear to be different colors when viewed under different types of light. Thin sections of volcanic glass from erupting volcanoes, for example, can appear tan, brown, or black when viewed in different lights.

Geologists also use light, in addition to other tools, to help them classify rocks according to their structure and how they were formed.

Geologists cut a very thin section of a rock in order to study it. Pictured here is a thin section of garnet schist, a rock commonly found in New England.

## GEOARCHAEOLOGY

**Geoarchaeology** is the study of the rocks and landforms present in Earth's crust that impact archaeological sites, the remains of places where humans have lived in the past. Most geoarchaeologists collect rocks or minerals from these sites, and then examine those rocks in a laboratory to learn something about the people and culture that once thrived there.

A typical geoarchaeologist, for example, might study how soils buried ancient artifacts, how those soils preserved or destroyed human remains, or how soils helped spread or retain artifacts in the Earth's crust over time.

In one recent study published in the journal *Geoarchaeology*, for example, scientists collected ash from archeological sites in Scotland. They then studied the ash to determine what sorts of fuel sources—coal, peat, or oil—were used by ancient humans. In this case, the leftover rocks in the area helped explain how the people lived. The researchers found that a diverse array of fuel sources was used by people in the region.

## GEOCHEMISTRY

**Geochemistry** is the study of the chemical composition of the Earth and its many parts. Most geochemists will measure and study chemicals taken from rocks found at Earth's surface. But these rocks may have been formed in the lower mantle, the upper mantle, or in the crust itself. Which Earth layer a geochemist studies depends on where the rocks being studied were formed.

An isotope geochemist, for example, uses the **isotopes** found in rocks to study Earth's crust. An element can come in different forms called isotopes. Each isotope contains a different number of particles at the center of the element, which the element loses in a predictable way. Counting the number of particles in the isotope form of an element helps scientists determine the age of the element.

Geochemists use the isotopes in rocks to determine the age of Earth's crust. The isotopes found in ice help determine amounts of pollution in past time periods. The isotopes in archaeological artifacts help establish the age of ruins. The isotopes in groundwater help measure its age.

## GEOCHRONOLOGY

**Geochronology** is the science of determining the age of crustal rocks, minerals, fossils, and sediments and putting them in order in the history of the Earth to create a detailed and reliable timeline. Most geochronologists collect samples on Earth's surface, determine the age of the samples in the laboratory, and then piece together the history of a particular event.

A tephrochronologist, for example, is a geochronologist who specializes in volcanic ash deposits. When a volcano erupts, it often sends rocks and ash thousands of miles away. A tephrochronologist can collect and date this ash to help determine how and when a particular volcano erupted.

Geochronologists use many methods to determine the ages of rocks. Isotope geochemistry, fossil information, and the magnetic orientation of minerals in rocks are just a few of them. Geochronology often uses chemistry, but it always uses the measurements of time.

## Geodesy

**Geodesy**, also called geodetics, is the study of the shape of the Earth and the points on its surface. Geodesy specialists really study all of Earth's layers together; they aren't so interested in differences of processes within the separate layers, but in the Earth's interior structure and shape as a whole. Early geodetics used telescopes and math to make observations and measurements of the Earth. Today, most modern geodetics uses GPS instruments.

GPS instruments communicate with a network of satellites that orbit the Earth. The satellites help determine the exact location of a GPS instrument anchored to one spot on the surface of the planet. Over time, very small movements of the instrument can be detected and recorded by the satellites. GPS systems are widely used today.

For example, the U.S. Department of Defense, the U.S. federal agency charged with defending the country, operates 21 GPS satellites in space. According to the USGS, the federal GPS system monitors the movements of tectonic plates in the Pacific Ocean so that scientists can better understand the events leading up to earthquakes and volcanic eruptions.

These geologists are at work installing GPS equipment and seismometers near Mount Erebus, the most active volcano in Antarctica. This kind of monitoring equipment allows scientists to study seismic activity, as well as gain advance warnings of possible eruptions.

## GEOHYDROLOGY

**Geohydrology**, or hydrogeology, is the study of groundwater movements in the crust of the Earth. Most geohydrologists, therefore, are experts in two fields of science: the geology of Earth's crust and the physics of water movement.

A typical task of a geohydrologist is to predict the behavior of an aquifer. An **aquifer** is an underground body of water that can be extracted for human use. (Wells have access to aquifers but are not themselves a type of aquifer.)

Many aquifers are composed of porous rock, or rock that has a lot of holes in it, like a sponge. A geohydrologist's job is to figure out how water, and sometimes contaminants, move in underground rocks and how to best extract the water for human use.

## GEOMORPHOLOGY

**Geomorphology** is the study of the shape of the land on the surface of Earth's crust. Most geomorphologists spend time looking at maps of the Earth, studying landforms, and examining the rocks contained in those landforms.

A structural geologist, for example, is a geomorphologist who studies how rocks are distributed on Earth's surface—how they are layered, folded, flattened, or shaped. They help explain why a patch of land looks the way it looks, and what may be hiding beneath the crust.

Economically valuable rocks and minerals are often found in the crust. Oil and coal are often mined and sold, for use as an energy source. A structural geologist can help locate deposits of economically valuable rocks like coal, and give companies advice on the best way to get them out of the ground.

## GEOPHYSICS

**Geophysics** uses physics to study the inner layers of the Earth including the upper and lower mantle and the inner and outer core. Geophysicists study how waves of energy travel through the Earth, including waves associated with earthquakes and volcanoes. There are two types of seismology used by most geophysicists: active and passive.

Active seismologists create shaking events that deliberately send energy through the Earth at specific locations. An active seismologist might set off a small explosion, for example, to shake the Earth and record the seismic waves.

Passive seismologists wait for natural shaking events to occur. A passive seismologist might wait for an earthquake in California, for example, to learn more about the San Andreas Fault.

Active seismologists have the advantage of creating energy waves where and when they want them. But this can be expensive, and covers only a limited area. Passive seismologists have to wait for shaking events to take place in certain locations to

# GIS Mapping

As Earth scientists learn more and more about the planet Earth, it becomes a challenge to just keep up with all the information and new discoveries. Geographic Information System technology, or GIS, is a growing field of science that attempts to make sense of it all.

GIS technology manages information and displays it visually, usually in the form of a map. When applied to the Earth sciences, GIS combines Earth science information, or data, with a computer's ability to display and search that data, creating very powerful research tools.

Earth science and GIS combine in many different ways. One way is through the use of space satellites designed for Earth observation. The information collected by satellites can be fed directly into GIS software to produce maps of the Earth's surface, atmosphere, or subsurface, ultimately creating maps that are based on accurate scientific measurements.

Over time, scientists can compare these maps to learn about how the Earth is changing. The growth of vegetation in a particular region on Earth, for example, can be mapped over the course of a growing season. From such GIS maps, Earth scientists can learn how drought and rainfall impacted an area and come up with a rough measure of plant growth.

GIS technology continues to grow and be used in new ways. In fact, people with GIS skills usually have no problems finding well-paying, interesting jobs related to the Earth sciences.

conduct their studies. But these events do not cost anything or require extra work to create. Each of these events is useful to seismologists in different ways.

## EARTH SCIENCE EDUCATION

To prepare for a career studying the layers of the Earth takes some planning. Some high schools offer Earth or environmental science classes that can be good places to start. Increasingly, opportunities for more involved Earth science projects are available for students and teachers.

Part of the federally funded EarthScope project, for example, is to make Earth science research more accessible in schools. EarthScope has developed a handful of teaching tools covering Earth's volcanoes and earthquakes. For example, an animation program about Alaska's St. Augustine volcano shows the processes taking place in the mountain and how they relate to plate tectonics. In the future, EarthScope hopes to make its many monitoring instruments and discoveries directly accessible online to students.

Such specific Earth science projects are fun, but there is no replacing a basic science education. Julie Elliott, a Ph.D. student at the University of Alaska-Fairbanks, encourages students interested in Earth science careers to "take lots of math, physics (particularly mechanics), geology, and computer science classes." Elliott also says, "Learn how to write. The ability to write well is an invaluable tool for a scientist."

## THE ULTIMATE GOAL: UNDERSTANDING EARTH'S LAYERS

Earth's dynamic layers do not move and change for no reason. There are forces, processes, and explanations for why the planet acts as it does. In recent decades, scientists have discovered much about Earth's layers, but the crustal earthquakes, mantle-rooted volcanoes, and magnetic flips of Earth's core still provide unsolved mysteries for modern scientists.

Future solutions to these mysteries will help scientists predict changes in Earth's layers that could help save lives. A city could be warned before a major earthquake occurs; villagers could prepare for a nearby volcanic eruption; and satellites could be adjusted for changes in Earth's magnetic field. There is good reason to understand and learn about the Earth's dynamic layers.

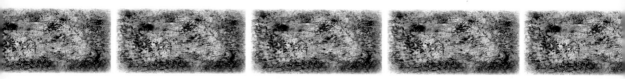

# Glossary

▲

**Aquifer**   An underground body of water that can be extracted for human use.

**Asthenosphere**   The lowermost part of the mantle; made of liquid rock.

**Basalts**   Gray or black, fine-textured, heavy rocks that are squeezed out of underwater volcanoes.

**Compression**   Stress that pushes Earth's crust together, squeezing it until it folds or breaks.

**Continental crust**   The layer of crust that forms the land and is made largely of rocks called granite.

**Continental drift**   The idea that Earth's continents float around the surface of the planet and were once a single piece of land. The precursor to plate tectonics.

**Convection**   The movement of heat within a liquid.

**Convergent boundary**   Area where two plates are moving toward each other, or converging, and Earth's crust is being destroyed.

**Crystal**   An organized solid with its parts packed in specific patterns.

**Direct science**   The type of science that uses real, concrete examples that can be observed, measured, and studied with the human eye.

**Divergent boundary**   An area where two plates are moving away from each other, or diverging, and new crust is being created.

**Earth science**   The study of planet Earth.

**Earthquake**   When the crust of the Earth moves and cracks.

**Element**   A substance that cannot be reduced to a simpler substance by normal chemical means.

**Fault**   A break in Earth's crust.

**Fault-block mountain**   A type of mountain created when two normal faults line up next to each other in the Earth.

**Geoarchaeology**   The study of the rocks and landforms that impact archaeological sites, places where humans have lived in the past.

**Geochemistry**   The study of the chemical composition of the Earth and its many parts.

**Geochronology**   The science of determining the age of rocks, minerals, fossils, and sediments and putting them in order in the history of the Earth, making a detailed and reliable timeline.

**Geodesy**   The study of the shape of the Earth and points on its surface; also called geodetics.

**Geodynamo**   The mechanism at Earth's core that creates the magnetic field of the Earth.

**Geohydrology**   The study of groundwater movements in the crust of the Earth; also called hydrogeology.

**Geology**   The study of the solid matter in the Earth, including the history and processes that shape the planet's rocks, soils, oils, and gemstones.

**Geomorphology**   The study of the shape of the land.

**Geophysics**   Uses physics to study movements of the Earth, including the plate movements associated with earthquakes and volcanoes.

**Geothermal** Heat that comes from inside the Earth.

**GPS (Global Positioning System)** A network of satellites in space that are used to determine precise locations on Earth's surface.

**Granites**   Pink, gray, or black rocks that have melted and solidified on Earth's surface over time.

**Gravitational heat**   Heat created when rocks scrape and slide past each other inside the Earth due to the force of gravity.

**Gravity**   The force of attraction between two things that have mass, or weight.

**Heat**   A form of energy created by tiny movements of particles inside the elements.

**Hot spot**   An area where large amounts of new crust are created.

**Indirect science**   The type of science that uses tools and instruments to look and listen without direct observation.

**Isotope**   An isotope contains a different number of particles at the center of the element, which the element loses in a predictable way.

**Kimberlite pipe**   A specialized volcano that often brings diamonds and other rocks from deep in the upper mantle to Earth's surface.

**Lithosphere**   The solid, outermost shell of Earth.

**Magma**   Liquid rock that supplies lava for a volcano.

**Magnetic field**   A force that causes the tiny particles inside elements to line up in predictable and patterned ways.

**Magnetic variation**   The direction that magnetic minerals within a rock are pointing.

**Meteorites**   Objects from outer space that impact the Earth.

**Mid-ocean ridge**   An underwater mountain range where the Earth's crust is moving apart and new oceanic rocks are coming to the surface.

**Normal fault**   When tension forces stretch the crust apart.

**Oceanic crust**   The layer of crust beneath the oceans that is made of basalts.

**Peridotites**   Crustal rocks that make up the lithosphere of the upper mantle.

**Photon**   A particle of light.

**Planetesimals**   Rocky elements that stuck together to form larger planets and asteroids after the creation of the universe.

**Plate boundaries**   The edges of the plates on Earth's surface.

**Plate tectonics**   A scientific theory to explain the location of continents on Earth's surface and how they move.

**Plates**   The moving pieces of Earth's crust.

**P waves**   Seismic waves that compress and stretch the Earth from side to side like an accordion in the direction they are traveling; also known as primary waves.

**Radioisotope**   A special form of an element that is radioactive.

**Rift**   A place where Earth's crust is being pulled apart.

**Seafloor spreading**   The spreading apart of Earth's crust at mid-ocean ridges to form new rocks.

**Seismology**   The study of waves of energy traveling through the Earth.

**Shearing**   Stress that pushes a piece of rock in two opposite directions, causing a break or change of shape.

**Silicates**   A type of rock, usually containing the elements silicon and oxygen.

**Stress**   A force that acts on the crust to change its shape, size, and location.

**Strike/slip fault**   When shearing forces pull rock in opposite directions.

**Subduction zone**   An area where heavy oceanic crust is sucked back inside the Earth, destroying the old crust.

**S waves**   Seismic waves that move in two directions, from side to side and up and down; also known as shear waves.

**Tension**   Stress that stretches the crust apart, making it thinner in the middle.

**Thrust fault**   When compression forces smash the crust together.

**Transform boundary**   A place where two plates slip and slide past each other, moving in opposite directions. Here, crust is neither destroyed nor made.

**Weathering**   The breaking down of rocks on Earth's surface by wind, water, heat, and pressure.

# Bibliography

▲

American Museum of Natural History. "The Nature of Diamonds," AMNH Web site. Available online. Accessed July 24, 2008. URL: http://www.amnh.org/exhibitions/diamonds/index.html.

Anuta, Joe. "Probing Question: What Heats Earth's Core?" Penn State University Web site. Available online. Accessed July 24, 2008. URL: http://www.rps.psu.edu/probing/earth.html.

Arizona State University. "New Picture of Earth's Lower Mantle," *ScienceDaily* Web site. Available online. Accessed July 24, 2008. URL: http://www.sciencedaily.com/releases/2007/06/070621140813.htm.

British Broadcasting Corporation News. "Legendary US Landmark Falls Down," BBC News Web site. Available online. Accessed July 24, 2008. URL: http://news.bbc.co.uk/1/hi/world/americas/2999233.stm.

Broad, William J. "Earth's Inner Core Rotates At Faster Rate Than Surface," *New York Times* Web site. Available online. Accessed July 24, 2008. URL: http://query.nytimes.com/gst/fullpage.html?res=9D05E2DB1F39F93BA25754C0A960958260&sec=&spon=&pagewanted=print.

Broecker, Wallace. *How to Build a Habitable Planet.* New York: ELDIGIO Press, 1985.

California Geological Survey. "California Has Its Faults," CGS Web site. Available online. Accessed July 24, 2008. URL: http://www.consrv.ca.gov/cgs/information/publications/teacher_features/faults.htm.

Church, M.J., C. Peters, and C.M. Batt. "Sourcing fire ash on archaeological sites in the Western and Northern Isles of Scotland,
using mineral magnetism," *Geoarchaeology* Web site. Available
online. Accessed July 24, 2008. URL: http://www3.interscience.
wiley.com/cgi-bin/abstract/116310342/ABSTRACT.

EarthScope. "Observatories," EarthScope Web site. Available
online. Accessed July 24, 2008. URL: http://www.earthscope.
org/index.php/es_obs.

EarthScope Education and Outreach Bulletin. "Activity at Augustine
Volcano," EarthScope Web site. Available online. Accessed July
24, 2008. URL: http://www.earthscope.org/es_doc/eno/TM1.
pdf.

Elliott, Julie. Personal communication. October 4–7, 2007.

Fortey, Richard. *Earth: An Intimate History.* New York: Vintage
Books, Random House, 2005.

Glatzmaier, Gary A. "Gary A. Glatzmaier," University of California
Santa Cruz Web site. Available online. Accessed July 24, 2008.
URL: http://www.es.ucsc.edu/~glatz/index.html.

Hawaii Center for Volcanology. "Mauna Loa Volcano," HCV Web
site. Available online. Accessed July 24, 2008. URL: http://
www.soest.hawaii.edu/GG/HCV/maunaloa.html.

Ince, Martin. *The Rough Guide to The Earth.* New York: Rough
Guides, The Penguin Group, 2007.

Integrated Ocean Drilling Program. "IODP Brochure," IODP
Web site. Available online. Accessed July 24, 2008. URL:
http://www.iodp.org/media-kit/.

International Union of Pure and Applied Chemistry. "IUPAC
Periodic Table of the Elements," IUPAC Web site. Available
online. Accessed July 24, 2008. URL: http://www.iupac.org/
reports/periodic_table/IUPAC_Periodic_Table-3Oct05.pdf.

Mount St. Helens National Volcanic Monument Web site.
Available online. Accessed July 24, 2008. URL: http://www.
fs.fed.us/gpnf/mshnvm/.

Nordlys, Northern Lights. "What Causes Them?" Nordlys Web site. Available online. Accessed July 24, 2008. URL: http://www.northern-lights.no/english/what/cause.shtml.

Reed, Christina. "Old Man of the Mountain," *Geotimes* Web site. Available online. Accessed July 24, 2008. URL: http://www.geotimes.org/may03/WebExtra050503.html.

Roach, John. "Earth's Magnetic Field is Fading," *National Geographic* Web site. Available online. Accessed July 24, 2008. URL: http://news.nationalgeographic.com/news/2004/09/0909_040909_earthmagfield.html.

Schwartz, Mark. Stanford University News. "Stanford, U.S. Geological Survey team up to get inside scoop on quake zone," Stanford University Web site. Available online. Accessed July 24, 2008. URL: http://news-service.stanford.edu/news/2003/december3/safod-123.html.

Scientific American. "Ask the Experts: Geology," *Scientific American* Web site. Available online. Accessed July 24, 2008. URL: http://www.sciam.com/askexpert_question.cfm?articleID=00006E21-C156-1C71-9EB7809EC588F2D7.

Stevenson, David. "A Modest Proposal: Mission to Earth's Core," California Institute of Technology Web site. Available online. Accessed July 24, 2008. URL: http://www.planetary.caltech.edu/faculty/stevenson/coremission/index.html.

Stevenson, David J. "David J. Stevenson," California Institute of Technology Web site. Available online. Accessed July 24, 2008. URL: http://www.planetary.caltech.edu/faculty/stevenson/.

Than, Ker. "Earth's Core Rotates Faster than Surface, Study Confirms," LiveScience Web site. Available online. Accessed July 24, 2008. URL: http://www.livescience.com/environment/050825_earthcore.html.

United States Geological Survey. "Cinder Cones," USGS Web site. Available online. Accessed July 24, 2008. URL: http://volcanoes.usgs.gov/Products/Pglossary/CinderCone.html.

United States Geological Survey. "Inside the Earth," USGS Web site. Available online. Accessed July 24, 2008. URL: http://pubs.usgs.gov/gip/dynamic/inside.html.

United States Geological Survey. "Understanding Plate Motions," USGS Web site. Available online. Accessed July 24, 2008. URL: http://pubs.usgs.gov/gip/dynamic/understanding.html.

United States Geological Survey. "USGS Announces that Augustine Volcano in Alaska Erupted Today," USGS Web site. Available online. Accessed July 24, 2008. URL: http://www.usgs.gov/newsroom/article.asp?ID=1427.

United States Geological Survey. "What Kind of Movement Has Occurred Along the Fault?," USGS Web site. Available online. Accessed July 24, 2008. URL: http://pubs.usgs.gov/gip/earthq3/move.html.

United States Geological Survey. "Yellowstone Caldera, Wyoming," USGS Web site. Available online. Accessed July 24, 2008. URL: http://vulcan.wr.usgs.gov/Volcanoes/Yellowstone/description_yellowstone.html.

University of Alaska-Fairbanks. "Augustine Eruption Leads to Updated Model," UAF Web site. Available online. Accessed July 24, 2008. URL: http://www.uaf.edu/news/featured/07/augustine/.

University of Texas at El Paso. "The Landscape, the Animals, the Plants," UTEP Web site. Available online. Accessed July 24, 2008. URL: http://museum.utep.edu/chih/theland/landscape/landscape.htm.

# Further Reading

▲

## BOOKS

Erickson, John. *Plate Tectonics: Unraveling the Mysteries of the Earth*. New York: Facts on File Science Library, 2001.

Gates, Alexander. *Encyclopedia of Earthquakes and Volcanoes*. New York: Facts on File Science Library, 2006.

Goldberg, Jan. *Earth Imaging Satellites*. New York: Chelsea House, 2003.

Krysac, L.C. *Gravitational, Electric and Magnetic Forces: An Anthology of Current Thought*. New York: Rosen Central, 2005.

Lambert, David. *The Field Guide to Geology*. New York: Checkmark Books, 2006.

Monier, Eric M. *How Life on Earth Is Affected by Earth's Unique Placement and Orientation in Our Solar System*. New York: Rosen Central, 2006.

O'Neil Grace, Catherine. *Forces of Nature: The Awesome Power of Volcanoes, Earthquakes, and Tornadoes*. Washington D.C.: National Geographic Children's Books, 2004.

Vogel, Carole G. and Michael Wysession. *Science Explorer: Inside Earth*. Boston: Pearson Prentice Hall, 2007.

## WEB SITES

**American Museum of Natural History: Our Dynamic Planet**
http://www.amnh.org/education/resources/rfl/web/
    earthmag/index.htm
*An accurate look at a few fun Earth processes for young readers.*

**CNN: Layers of the Earth**
http://www.cnn.com/interactive/nature/9903/earth.layers/
    frameset.exclude.html
*An animated, interactive tour through Earth's layers.*

**EarthScope: Did You Know?**
http://www.dpc.ucar.edu/earthscopeVoyager/JVV_Jr/
    didyouknow/index.html
*Provides scientific background on some geologic features on the North American continent.*

**KidsGeo.com**
http://www.kidsgeo.com/index.php
*A kid-friendly site focused on geology and geography.*

**National Aeronautics and Space Administration, Jet Propulsion Laboratory**
**The Southern California Integrated GPS Network Education Module**
http://scign.jpl.nasa.gov/learn/index.htm
*An academic site focused on understanding Earth's plate motions.*

**Public Broadcasting Service: Savage Earth**
http://www.pbs.org/wnet/savageearth/animations/
    hellscrust/main.html
*An animation of some structural features inside the Earth.*

**U.S. Geological Survey: USGS Volcano Hazards Program**
http://volcanoes.usgs.gov
*The USGS's Volcanic Hazards Program pages. Includes information on recent volcanic activity on Earth.*

# Photo Credits

▲

# Index

▲

**A**

Alaska Volcano Observatory (AVO), 51
Appalachian Mountains, 22, 26
aquifers, 83–84
asthenosphere, 30
Augustine volcano. *See* St. Augustine, Mount
aurora australis, 62–63
aurora borealis, 62–63
AVO (Alaska Volcano Observatory), 51

**B**

basalts, 16, 19
basins, 22
boundaries of plates. *See* plate boundaries

**C**

cinder cones, 48
Colorado Plateau, 23
compasses, 64–65
composite volcanoes (stratovolcanos), 48–49
compression, 22
computer modeling, 67
continental crust, 19, 21–22
continental drift, 33
convection
  in lower mantle, 45–47
  and plate movements, 37
  in upper mantle, 31–33, 37
convergent boundary, 40

core, 10, 15. *See also* inner core; outer core
core expansion, 74
core samples, seafloor, 46
crust, 10, 18–28
  age, 19–22
  continental, 19, 21–22
  earthquakes and, 18, 24–28
  faults, 24–28
  forces in, 22–23
  formation of, 16
  ingredients, 19
  oceanic, 19–20
  thickness, 19
crustal graveyard, 44, 56–57
crystal structure of inner core, 75

**D**

D" layer, 56–57, 58
dating of rocks, isotopes for, 11–12, 81
diamonds, 30–31
direct science, 11–12
divergent boundary, 40
drilling, seafloor, 46

**E**

Earth
  continental plates of, 36–37
  formation of, 12–16, 74
  layers of, overview, 9–11, 13–17. *See also* core; crust; mantle
  magnetic field of. *See* magnetic field

Earth science, 11, 78–87
  education in, 86
  geoarchaeology, 80–81
  geochemistry, 81
  geochronology, 81–82
  geodesy, 82
  geohydrology, 83–84
  geology, 79
  geomorphology, 84
  geophysics, 26, 84–86
  goals of, 86–87
  scientific methods used in,
    11–12
earthquakes, 9
  faults and, 24–28
  prediction of, 28
  in shaping of crust, 18
  transform boundaries and, 41,
    43
EarthScope, 26–27, 54–55, 86
education in Earth science, 86
electricity, 64, 71, 74–77
elements, 11
Elliott, Julie, 42, 86

**F**
fault-block mountain, 24
faults, 24–28
  normal faults, 24
  San Andreas Fault, 27–28, 41,
    43
  strike/slip faults, 26–28
  thrust faults, 25–26
Franklin Mountains, 24
Freymueller, Jeff, 54

**G**
Gauss, Carl Friedrich, 66–67
geoarchaeology, 80–81
geochemistry, 81
geochronology, 81–82
geodesy, 82
geodetics, 82
geodynamos, 64, 67
Geographic Information System
  (GIS) mapping, 85
geohydrology, 83–84

geology, 79
geomorphology, 84
geophysics, 26, 84–86
geothermal heat, 71
GIS (Geographic Information
  System) mapping, 85
Glatzmaier, Gary, 67
Global Positioning System
  (GPS)
  in geodesy, 82
  in plate tectonic research, 42
  in study of volcanoes, 50,
    52–55
granites, 16, 19
gravitational heat, 72–73
gravity, outer core and, 61
Great Basin, 22
Great Rift Valley, 40

**H**
Hawaii, 38
Hawaiian Island chain, 49
heat, in outer core, 61
heat production, 69, 71–74
Himalayan Mountains, 40
hot spots, 38
hot spot volcanoes, 49
hydrogeology, 83–84
hydrophones, 53

**I**
Iceland, 38
indirect science, 12
inner core, 10, 69–77
  age, 70
  electricity of, 74–77
  forces in, 70–71
  formation of, 15
  heat of, 69, 71–74
  ingredients, 70
  rotation of, 69–70
  thickness, 70
Integrated Ocean Drilling
  Program (IODP), 46
iron, in core, 15, 60, 64,
  70–71
isotopes, 11–12, 81

**K**

kimberlite pipes, 31

**L**

lithosphere, 19, 30
lower mantle, 10, 44–58
    age, 45
    convection in, 45–47
    crustal graveyard, 44,
      56–57
    formation of, 15–16
    ingredients, 45
    methods for study of, 50–55
    thickness, 45
    volcanoes and. *See* volcanoes

**M**

magma, 9
magnetic field, 61–68
    auroras and, 62–63
    geodynamos and, 64, 67
    pointing direction of, 64–65
    pole reversals of, 66–67
    production of, 59–60, 64
    properties of, 61–63
    protective effects of, 59–60,
      65–66
magnetic variation, 34
magnetism, of seafloor, 34–35
mantle, 10. *See also* lower mantle;
  upper mantle
    formation of, 15–16
    heat production in, 71, 72–73
mantle plumes, 49
marine seismology, 52–53
Mauna Loa, 48
meteorites, 14
Mid-Atlantic Ridge, 38
mid-ocean ridges, 34, 38, 40, 52
moon, 72–73
Mount St. Augustine. *See* St.
  Augustine, Mount
Mount St. Helens, 49
mountain formation, 22, 24, 40
movement of plates, 37

**N**

normal faults, 24
northern lights, 62–63

**O**

ocean floor. *See* seafloor
oceanic crust, 19–20
"Old Man of the Mountain,"
  20–21
olivine, 30
outer core, 10, 59–68
    age, 61
    forces in, 61
    formation of, 15
    ingredients, 60
    magnetic field of. *See* magnetic
      field
    thickness, 60

**P**

P waves, 52, 57–58
Paricutin, 48
peridotites, 30
perovskite, 45
photons, 63
planetary science, 76
planetesimals, 15
planets
    auroras of, 63
    computer modeling of, 67
    Earth-like, 14
plate boundaries, 38–43
    convergent, 40
    divergent, 40
    transform, 41–43
Plate Boundary Observatory, 54
plate tectonics, 29, 33–43
    history, 33–36
    plate boundaries, 38–43
    plate movements, 37
    plates, 36–37
    process of, 43
plateaus, 23
plates, 36–37
pointing direction of magnetic
  field, 64–65
pole reversals, 66–67
primary waves. *See* P waves

**R**

radioactive dating, 11–12
radioactivity, geothermal heat
  and, 71

radioisotopes, 11
radiometric dating, 11–12
rift valleys, 24, 40
rifts, 24
Rio Grande Rift, 24
river valleys. *See* rift valleys
rocks, dating of, 11–12, 81
Rocky Mountains, 26

**S**
S waves, 52, 57–58
San Andreas Fault, 27–28, 41,
   43
San Andreas Fault Observatory at
   Depth (SAFOD), 26–27, 54
San Francisco earthquake, 43
San Gabriel Mountains, 26
seafloor
   drilling of, 46
   magnetism of, 34–35
   spreading of, 34
secondary waves. *See* S waves
seismic waves, 52–53, 57–58
seismographs, 12, 13
seismology, 12, 44
   basic principles of, 57–58
   in geophysics, 84–86
   inner core studies, 74–75
   marine, 52–53
   in study of volcanoes, 51
   USArray project, 55
   volcanic studies, 50
shear waves. *See* S waves
shearing, 22–23
shield volcanoes, 47–48
silicates, 15
solar wind, 60, 62–63,
   65–66
southern lights, 62–63
St. Augustine, Mount
   2006 eruption, 7–9
   GPS on, 53–55
   seismology of, 51
St. Helens, Mount, 49
Stevenson, David J., 76
stratovolcanos, 48–49

stress, 22
strike/slip faults, 26–28
structural geologists, 84
subduction zones, 8, 20, 40

**T**
T waves, 53
tectonic plates, 36–37
tension, 22
tephrochronologists, 82
tertiary waves. *See* T waves
thrust faults, 25–26
Tolstoy, Maya, 52–53
transform boundary, 41–43

**U**
United States Array (USArray),
   55
upper mantle, 10, 29–43. *See also*
   plate tectonics
   age, 30–31
   convection in, 31–33, 37
   formation of, 15–16
   ingredients, 30
   plate movements and, 37
   thickness, 30
USArray (United States Array),
   55

**V**
valley formation, 22
volcanoes, 44, 47–55. *See also*
   Augustine volcano
   prediction of eruptions, 50
   study methods, 50–55
   subduction zones and, 8–9
   types of, 47–49

**W**
weathering, 20
Wegener, Alfred, 33–34

**Y**
Yellowstone National Park, 49

**Z**
Zoback, Mark, 26–27

# About the Author

▲

**KRISTA WEST** has written about Earth science for parents and young adults for nearly 10 years. Growing up at the foot of the Cascade Mountains in Washington State, Krista was always aware of the moving mountains and living land around her. But only when she entered graduate school in New York did Krista begin to understand the inner layers of the planet. She has an M.A. in Earth science and an M.S. in journalism, both from Columbia University.